NEW DIRECTIONS IN MODERN ECONOMICS
Series Editor: Malcolm C. Sawyer,
Professor of Economics, University of Leeds, UK

New Directions in Modern Economics presents a challenge to orthodox economic thinking. It focuses on new ideas emanating from radical traditions including post-Keynesian, Kaleckian, neo-Ricardian and Marxian. The books in the series do not adhere rigidly to any single school of thought but attempt to present a positive alternative to the conventional wisdom.

A list of published titles in this series is printed at the end of this volume.

Financial Liberalization and Intervention

A New Analysis of Credit Rationing

Santonu Basu

NEW DIRECTIONS IN MODERN ECONOMICS

Edward Elgar
Cheltenham, UK • Northampton, MA, USA

Published by
Edward Elgar Publishing Limited
Glensanda House
Montpellier Parade
Cheltenham
Glos GL50 1UA
UK

Edward Elgar Publishing, Inc.
136 West Street
Suite 202
Northampton
Massachusetts 01060
USA

A catalogue record for this book
is available from the British Library

ISBN   1 84064 965 8

Typeset by Cambrian Typesetters, Frimley, Surrey
Printed and bound in Great Britain by MPG Books Ltd, Bodmin, Cornwall

Contents

Preface

This book examines why the policy of financial liberalization and for that matter financial intervention, were unable to improve all borrowers' access to the loan market. It is argued that the loan market operates in the presence of uncertainty, and as a result, other than the interest rate, there are two additional factors, namely the credit standard and credit risk, that play a crucial role in determining borrowers' access to the loan market. Lenders introduce the credit standard in order to ensure that should the borrowers' projects for which they sought loans fail, there remains some alternative means to enable lenders to recoup their loan capital. The issue of credit risk principally arises because, in the competitive atmosphere in which this market operates, lenders are not able, in all circumstances, to secure their loans by the credit standard. The portion of the loan which is not secured by the credit standard is subject to credit risk. It is the variation in the credit standard implemented by the respective lenders which causes the variation in the access of different groups of borrowers to the loan market. Proponents of policies in the past as well as in the present investigated neither why lenders introduce the credit standard nor what causes the variation in the credit standard; instead they under-estimated or overlooked the importance of this issue. As a result both past and present policies either adversely affected the performance of this sector or brought about a crisis. This was at least the case for India and South Korea.

This is a brief description of my book. The idea of writing this book originated at the time my supervisor Associate Professor John Pullen, who has always been interested in my work, suggested that I put together my published and unpublished papers for a PhD degree. In an attempt to do this, the thesis became a further development of my thoughts that I had already published in *Economic Papers*, *Australian Economic Papers* and *World Development*. Then, as I was preparing my PhD dissertation, I thought why shouldn't I write this piece in the form of a book? I also would like to thank John for his valuable comments. My debt to my wife Melinda Hughes is no less; besides receiving her constant support, I am grateful to her for reading the entire manuscript meticulously and thank her for her useful comments. I have had many stimulating discussions with Dr Imtiaz Omar, Mr Neil Hart and Dr Indranil Dutta and they have suggested some important improvements. I must thank them for that. Dr Kunal Sen looked at parts of the early drafts, Assistant Professor Pundarik Pukhopadhaya and Dr Shipra Dasgupta also looked through the early drafts and I must thank them for their useful comments. Finally I would like to thank the University of New England, Australia for providing me with a generous scholarship which allowed me to relinquish my teaching commitments and concentrate entirely on the thesis and hence this book. In preparing the final version of this book, I have greatly benefited from the valuable comments that I received from Professor Philip Arestis, Professor Amit Bhadhuri, Professor Ajit Singh and Professor Malcolm Sawyer. Of course my special thanks go to Philip, who since I joined South Bank University, London, despite an extremely busy schedule, was always available whenever I sought his assistance while preparing the final draft of this book. Finally I must thank my publisher Edward Elgar, especially Ms Dymphna Evans, Mr Matthew Pitman, and Ms Susan Hammant for their encouraging help on editorial matters. None of those mentioned above is, of course, in any way responsible for the views I have expressed or for any errors which may remain.

Santonu Basu
January 2002, London

1. General introduction

The main objective of this book is to examine why the policy of financial liberalization and, for that matter, the policy of financial intervention, were unable to achieve the respective goals sought by each policy. An important question is why execution of the policy of financial liberalization led to financial crisis, while intervention either adversely affected the performance of the financial sector or brought fragility into the system (without their respective objectives necessarily being fulfilled). Policy prescribers by their nature always take a defensive role. There is a saying in India that if you do not know how to dance then blame the floor. Without exception policy prescribers did just that, i.e. they blamed the macroeconomic environment or corruption and nepotism when either policy failed to live up to its promises. There is no doubt, despite this colloquial Indian saying, that the uneven or rough surface of the floor can adversely affect the performance of the dancer, but when there remains a possibility that the floor can be adversely affected by the dance performance, then it is necessary to examine the floor in order to decide whether such a performance can be carried out on it.

The failure of economic policies in relation to the financial system perhaps arose from the fact that the policy makers did not give adequate attention to understanding how the system operates and why it operates the way it does. This problem perhaps arises from our overriding objective of studying economics with a view as to how to improve the economic well-being of all members of society. Consequently, we often place a greater effort on identifying the problem than on examining why such problems arise, and then search for a system or a policy that satisfies our moral conviction. The problem that arises from this way of formulating a policy is that the policy is formulated in the presence of an incomplete understanding in relation to how the market operates. Both past and present policies relating to our financial system, especially on the issue of credit rationing, suffer from this problem.

The issue of credit rationing is perhaps one of the most controversial areas in the literature on economic theory. The origin of this controversy principally arises owing to a conventional claim in economic theory that it is market forces that determine the price, and it is the price that governs the allocation of resources. This means in the case of the loan market it is the interest rate that should govern the allocation of loans, i.e. credit. Contrary to this claim, it is observed that in the case of the loan market this is not necessarily so. In fact, it is observed that in this case preferential treatment among its potential clients is a regular part of its standard practice. In short, in this market, price alone does not always clear the market. For example, it has long been noted that small firms, small farms, lower socio-economic groups and firms seeking to invest in venture capital without the backing of a large firm or assets, do not have the first claim on the banks' preference. This problem has been observed in developed as well as in developing countries.[1] The question is why is this so? As banks are the major contributors in the loan market, this book will mainly deal with the banks' lending problems.

It is now recognized that this market operates differently compared with those where the delivery of, and payment for, goods and services take place simultaneously. In the case of the loan market, the advancement and payment of loans do not take place simultaneously, which means an element of both risk and uncertainty enters into such transactions, and may give the impression that perhaps small firms, small farms, lower socio-economic groups and firms seeking to invest in venture capital, offer a higher risk compared with other borrowers. As a result they may have less access to the banks' lending market. But the puzzling problem is that observation reveals that banks do not always attempt to avoid risk and uncertainty. In fact, it is not altogether too uncommon for banks to engage in speculative activity. For example, a buoyant economy is normally accompanied by a surge in bank lending, where much of the loan capital is engaged in speculative activities. These are short-term loans, which the borrowers use to purchase assets in anticipation that they will make a windfall gain on changes in the price of assets. Thus a collapse of the asset prices causes instability in the banking system, as the banks incur bad debts. The speculation is not confined to expected changes in the price of assets or equity but also extends to expected changes in commodity prices. The 1982–83 financial crisis in Latin America was largely followed by a fall in commodity prices. This form of involvement in the speculative market by banks not only often becomes a hindrance to the development of the industrial sector when they advance large loans for speculative activities during boom periods, but is believed to have caused financial crises.[2]

In addition to this, there exists no hard evidence to suggest that the default rate of those groups of borrowers who have been denied loans by the banks, is high. In fact, contrary to this, the fragmentary evidence that does exist indeed suggests that their default rate is low. For example, in the county of Cleveland, UK, it was observed that those who had been denied loans by the banks received loans from the informal sector at a much higher interest rate, yet their default rate was much lower compared with the firms who received loans from the banks (Storey, 1982). Similarly Raj (1979) noted in the case of India that the Rural Credit Survey, which was conducted by the Reserve Bank of India in 1951–52, reported that only 10 percent or less of the total amount of loans advanced were found to be doubtful. In recent years a similar situation has also been observed, for example in the case of Bangladesh, where commercial banks refused loans to lower socio-economic groups. For this reason Professor Yunus established the Bangladesh Grameen Bank in 1983, which exclusively offers loans to the 'have nots'. This bank's interest rate is not low, yet the default rate is less than 2 percent (Ghatak, 1995). The Bangladesh Grameen Bank has now lent $1 billion to over two million borrowers. Also, Wydick (1999) noted that similar kinds of institutions were established in various sectors of the developing nations following the Bangladesh Grameen Bank's experience, for example in Bolivia, the Dominican Republic, Ghana, Guatemala, Nepal, Nigeria, the Philippines, Thailand, and Zimbabwe, and in all of these cases it was found that the repayment rate on loans approached 100 percent. Furthermore, in the case of Australia there were two independent studies conducted by Juttner and Bird (1976) and Renfrew *et al.* (1985), where both noted that small businesses had a particular problem in gaining access to the trading banks' loan market, while having easier access to the finance companies' loan market. This problem principally arose owing to their smaller asset value (Renfrew *et al.*, 1985). Also small businesses often did not accept the banks' loan capital because the terms and conditions for obtaining such loans were not acceptable to them. In fact what is remarkable about these studies is that none of the authors found that the denial of loans to these borrowers arose from the possibility of a higher default rate, but principally from the fact that they were either unable or unwilling to meet the banks' terms and conditions for obtaining loans. The principal problem was that they had assets of lower value.[3]

But there exists overwhelming evidence to suggest that they pay a far higher interest rate on average than those who have normal access to the banks' loan market. For example, it was revealed that in the USA, small businesses had to pay 3 to 6 percent more than the prime rate on borrowed capital from the bank (Thomson and Leyden, 1982). In Japan, small or medium sized firms had to pay 50 percent more interest on borrowed capital than the large firms (Caves and Uekusa, 1976). In the case of developing countries there are no available data on the cost of borrowing for small enterprises, prior to the introduction of various government-sponsored schemes. This may be because they had access neither to the banks nor to the private moneylenders, but mostly relied on their own savings with the remainder coming from their friends and relatives.

The reference to high interest rates is only made in relation to the rural credit market where the existence of a high and dispersed interest rate has been observed. The interest rate that has been observed not only varies from country to country, but the puzzling feature of this market is that it also varies between and within regions, and in particular depends on the borrowers' and lenders' relationship and the purpose of the loan. For example, Nisbet (1967) found in rural Chile the interest rate is often 360 percent, while Griffin (1974) found the interest rate in rural areas varies from 0 to 200 percent from one region to another in the Philippines. Similarly, in the case of India, Bhaduri (1973) and Prasad (1974) found in certain regions such as in West Bengal and Bihar that the interest rate is very high, while Bardhan and Rudra (1978) and Rudra (1992), who has done a more comprehensive study of this issue, found that the interest rate, although high, is not universally as high as that found by Bhaduri and Prasad. More interestingly they found the interest rate varied from 0 to 50 percent. In my own study (1997), I found the annual interest rate varied from 30 to 50 percent. Similarly, a recent study by Smith *et al.* (1999) also found in the Sindh province of Pakistan that the annual interest rate on average varied from 40 to 80 percent. The puzzling feature of this variation in the interest rate and the complications under which this market operates were not well understood in the past, and will be discussed with reference to India.[4]

What is important for our context is to recognize that these borrowers often have to pay a much higher interest rate than those who have access to the formal loan market. It is these borrowers' lesser access to the formal loan market and their payment of higher interest rates that not only concern the governments of developed nations but cause serious problems for developing nations.

In the case of developed nations this concern principally arises for the two following reasons: one is pure economic necessity, and the other is the democratic aspiration that individuals must have a choice as to how they wish to pursue their livelihood. Both of these are important in their own right. The importance of the first issue principally arises from the fact that by the late 1960s it was becoming increasingly clear that GDP growth rate was no longer simultaneously followed by employment growth rate. In other words, employment growth rate was falling behind GDP growth rate. This trend started even prior to the Second World War, and was eloquently captured by Robinson (1931) in two observations he made. One was Ford's reorganization of his factory floor in 1921, which allowed him to reduce the number of workers employed daily for the production of each car from sixteen to nine. The second example was a German potash firm which, without altering its level of output, reduced the number of workers from 50,000 to 20,000 between 1923 and 1927.[5]

However the speed of this trend was nowhere near that which was observed during the post-war years. This was largely due to rapid technological change. This change also started to segregate the labour market to a greater extent than that observed in the early 20th century. For those labourers who have a basic education and are technologically skilled, their demand in the job market continues to rise, while the demand for uneducated and unskilled labourers continues to fall. Furthermore, governments can no longer rely on large corporations to solve the unemployment problem, as they are the principal beneficiaries of this technological change. In recent years, it has also been observed that in the corporate world, the price of shares principally follows cost-cutting exercises, and this means that one cannot expect cooperation from the corporate sector for unemployment reduction programmes. Therefore, small business is seen as the engine of employment growth, in particular for the unskilled labour force. This is mainly because it is the small business sector in general which uses less advanced technology compared with its larger counterparts. Thus the growth in small businesses and the growth of the self-employed has become an important vehicle to solve part of the unemployment problem, especially for the unskilled labour force. But, as stated above, this growth has been hindered by their lack of access to the formal loan market and by the fact that they often have to pay higher interest rates per unit of loan compared with those who do have access to this market. This in turn reduces their net profit rate, thereby limiting their incentive to hire more labour. Furthermore, it has been increasingly recognized that this sector's instability principally arises from its frequent cash shortage problems,[6] which can only be remedied by improving its access to the formal loan market.

The second issue that has concerned the governments of developed nations is that the foundation of democratic society rests on (among other things) the alternative choices that a society can offer to its individual members. In the economic context this means the society must offer its individual members a choice from various alternative means of survival. Restricted access to the loan market for a certain section of society means the members of that section have one less option than members of other sections. This conflicts with the philosophy on which the ideals of democracy rest.

In the case of developing nations, their problems are somewhat more acute than those of developed nations. The developing nations that used to be colonies of the developed nations, received their independence shortly after the Second World War, mainly as a result of their rising nationalism, and had a big task to develop their respective nations. This task was magnified by the fact that the momentum of sweeping nationalism rested on big promises that were made at that time by their respective leaders. The promise was that independence would allow them to use their nation's resources, which previously had been siphoned off by their colonial masters, for their own development. In other words, these resources then could be used to improve the living conditions of all people, especially those who otherwise would continue to live in extreme poverty. This means the enlargement of the entitlement set[7] is necessary for people specifically from the poorer section of the community, without which the meaning of independence carries little weight, and in fact loses any relevance for them.

These countries therefore are first required either to develop or to improve the necessary infrastructure, which is the prerequisite for the development of the industrial, as well as the rural, sectors. Development of both of these sectors has been considered to be the founding pillar on which it is possible to enlarge the entitlement set for the people concerned. Development of the industrial, as well as the rural, sectors requires long-term loans for investment in fixed capital; and to improve the living conditions of the general masses, loans also have to be allocated to small farmers, small enterprises and artisans. This means the financial sector has a very important role to play.

The financial sector's main role therefore was to mobilize the nation's savings and to allocate these savings to the productive areas of the economy that were considered necessary for the nation's development. In the absence of a well-developed stock market and non-banking financial institutions (NBFI), banks were considered to be the main players for fulfilling such tasks. The commercial banks that were operating at that time, mainly advanced loans to the trade-oriented part of the economy and specialized in the provision of short-term or working capital loans, mostly in the form of cash-credit and overdraft facilities (against the hypothecation of marketable tangible assets). They offered loans neither to small enterprises nor to the rural sector. They were mainly operating in urban and industrial locations, their size of operation was small, and therefore they neither had the means nor the willingness to extend the large and long-term loans that were necessary for industrial development. Furthermore, a large part of the financial or money market remained outside the orbit of the formal market. This means these commercial banks first had to bring this market within the orbit of the formal money market, so that much of the nation's savings could be brought under its control.

The situation that is described above suggests that some degree of intervention is required in the operation of the financial markets in both developed and developing countries. But the nature and the level of intervention differs considerably in both. This difference principally arises because developing countries want to bypass the necessary evolutionary stages that developed countries have undergone. Thus in the developed countries, intervention took the form of correcting some of the defects that were thought to have arisen from market imperfection whereas, in the developing countries, the intervention took the form of reshaping and developing their financial markets, with the aim that the banks would assist the nation in fulfilling its development objectives. In order to closely study the impact of this form of intervention in developing countries, we will confine our investigation to the cases of India and South Korea.

Accordingly, in the case of developed countries, for example in the USA, the Securities Exchange Act of 1934 gave power to the Federal Reserve System to regulate lending for stock market speculation. Similarly in 1946, the Bank of England Act introduced selective credit controls in order to ensure that a certain amount of credit would be allocated to industry and trade.[8] The different types of regulations that have been adopted by different countries may have followed from their respective historical experiences and needs, but the important point to note here is that regulations were adopted in order to ensure that a certain amount of credit was allocated for productive purposes, thereby limiting the flow of credit that otherwise would have been engaged in speculative activity. In the case of small businesses, small farms and lower socio-economic groups, loan guarantee schemes[9] and the ceiling on interest rates were introduced in order to ensure that these groups of borrowers received bank loans at a cheaper rate.

In the case of developing nations, the magnitude of the intervention was on a larger scale. There was a need for intervention to both allocate loanable funds to selective sectors and under-privileged groups, and also to mobilize nations' savings that otherwise would remain either in the hands of the informal sector or in an unproductive form. Accordingly, in order to mobilize higher levels of savings, for example in India, banks were often encouraged to open branch facilities outside the metropolitan area, while in other countries, such as South Korea, the interest rate on deposits was raised to a very high level. In order to allocate loans for long-term projects, industrial banks, along with other institutions, were developed, while in order to provide credit to the rural sector, a variety of rural banks were established. Furthermore, when it was recognized that commercial banks were reluctant to cooperate fully with the respective governments, banks were nationalized, for example in India and South Korea. In addition to that, a quota system was introduced for the provision of loans in India in order to ensure that the priority sector received a certain percentage of loans. The priority sector comprised the rural sector and small borrowers. In South Korea, banks were nationalized and a discriminatory interest rate policy was introduced in order to ensure that their priority sectors (largely composed of export and export-related sectors) received loans at a cheaper rate. Furthermore, in the case of South Korea, the government often used a variety of coercive devices in order to ensure that loans were not provided to its least preferred sectors of the economy. The advancement of loans for speculative purposes was discouraged by both of these nations.

The main objective of the regulations that were introduced in the developed countries, was to protect their depositors' funds from the excesses of banks' speculative activities, and to fulfil the respective government's social objectives. In the case of developing countries, intervention took the form of fulfilling governments' economic and social objectives.

But adequate attention was not given to the issue that the fulfilment of social objectives may not be easily reconciled with the banks' principal objective of maximizing their own profitability. This is a conflict which will often emerge between the maximization of individual profit and the maximization of social benefit; in other words, as a result of a divergence between the private return and the social return. This is an issue, which although extremely important, largely falls outside the scope of this book. But the question still arises, whether these policies were formulated on the basis of any theoretical investigation of why banks are reluctant to offer loans to some groups of borrowers while they quite readily offer loans even to those who use such funds for speculative activity. In other words, why do rational profit maximizing bankers use a discriminatory lending policy?

In the absence of such analysis, the impact of these interventions on the banking sector and the difficulty that they may cause the monetary authority, were not foreseen. The effect of these interventions, as banks were then prohibited by regulation from advancing loans to certain areas of economic activity, was to create the opportunity for new institutions to form in order to capture that end of the loan market. This in turn caused banks' share of the loan market to fall, thereby also affecting the effectiveness of the traditional tools that had been used by the monetary authority in the past to control the money supply. This was mainly because these new institutions were not subject to the same regulations as the banks. Consequently, this caused a convergence of interest between commercial banks and the monetary authority and raised some serious concerns about the negative aspect of these regulations. Furthermore, policies that were implemented in order to promote the access of smaller borrowers to the loan market at a cheaper rate, largely remained ineffective and often adversely affected whatever limited access they may have had to this loan market in the past. Some serious doubts were also raised, in particular about the merits of the ceiling on interest rates as a vehicle to provide loans to these borrowers at a cheaper rate.[10] In the case of developing nations, the intervention adversely affected the banking sector's performance,[11] with no appreciable improvement being observed in the smaller borrowers' access to the formal loan market.[12]

The ineffectiveness of these interventions and their adverse impact on the banking sector led one country after another to deregulate its financial sector. The view was taken that government intervention itself distorts the determination of the price of loans, thereby adversely affecting not only the allocation of loans but also savings. Accordingly, it is argued that in the absence of intervention, market forces will determine the interest rate, which in turn will govern the allocation of loans. There is no doubt that the intervention produced an unsatisfactory result. But the recent experience of financial crisis in the various developing nations and the large number of bank failures in developed countries,[13] also raise doubts about the merits of the liberalization policy. The issue of regulation or intervention arose again in order to prevent financial crisis, as it similarly emerged (and was undertaken) following the Great Depression. The important issue that arose from these experiences is that both policies, i.e. the policy of intervention and the policy of liberalization, were implemented with the objective of improving all borrowers' access to the loan market, specially those who are engaged in the productive aspect of the economy. In this respect both have failed, as neither of these policies was able to improve borrowers' access to the loan market in any sustainable manner. Thus the question is, where did they go wrong?

In order to address this issue, we need to examine why the interest rate alone does not clear the loan market. In other words, the question is, when two individuals or firms are prepared to pay the price, why does one receive the loan as demanded, while the other either receives less than what he/she demanded or is denied a loan altogether by banks? To put it more precisely, why do banks ration credit to some borrowers while meeting the demand of others? An analysis of this may allow us to understand why financial liberalization, and for that matter, the form of intervention that has been implemented in the past, were unable to improve all borrowers' access to the loan market, irrespective of their size.

In order to study these issues, the remainder of this book is divided into six chapters. In Chapter 2 we critically examine the existing literature on credit rationing with the specific intention of finding out whether this literature can shed some light on the above issue, i.e. why banks ration credit to some borrowers while they quite willingly meet the demands of others. It will be argued that despite its enormity and richness, this literature is somewhat limited in its ability to assist in the investigation of this specific issue. This is mainly because the existing literature investigates the rationing phenomenon that may have arisen due to particular circumstances in a specific situation. For example, authors investigate why the ceiling on interest rates causes banks to ration credit to some borrowers, or why the supply of loans is not monotonically related to the interest rate. Thus the investigation is confined within a specific context, and has not been extended to an examination of whether rationing is a generalized feature of the operation of this market; for example, when banks deny loans to some, why they quite willingly advance loans to others, even when they know that these borrowers may use such funds for speculative purposes. In other words, this literature has not investigated the rationing phenomenon by taking into account both aspects of banks' behaviour, i.e. by taking account of the character of the entire market's operation. In other words, why is it that for some groups of borrowers in the loan market banks appear to not be concerned about the risk and uncertainty, while for other groups they seem to be unwilling to take any risk and uncertainty? Furthermore, there is the question of, when banks deny loans to borrowers, why these borrowers receive loans from other lenders. The theoretical argument is at odds with this reality, as it argues that denial of loans to some borrowers by a bank provides a signal (or information) to other lending institutions about the risk aspect of those borrowers, and argues as a result these borrowers would not receive loans from other lenders.[14] But the observations by Juttner and Bird (1976) and Storey (1982) reveal that those who were denied loans by banks indeed received loans from other finance companies. In fact, a variety of private lending institutions have been developed to capture this end of the market. An example is the Bangladesh Grameen Bank. This issue becomes even more complicated in the context of the rural credit market where we find that the poorest borrowers who have been denied loans by all lenders, including banks, receive loans from their own landlords. Why is this so? In the absence of an investigation of these issues our understanding of the rationing phenomenon to some extent remains incomplete.

In Chapter 3 we explore how the loan market operates in the presence of uncertainty. The foundation of conventional theory is rested on the certainty assumption. In such a theory there is no room for uncertainty. Thus when the issue of uncertainty, or for that matter expectation, has arisen following Keynes (1936), it has been addressed within the framework of what is referred to as 'certainty equivalence'.[15] 'Certainty equivalence' in its crudest form is defined as a situation when an agent (i.e. an entrepreneur) acts as if his or her expectation is true (or certain), although this expectation is formed from a bundle of vague and various possibilities. In the statistical sense, this means the agent undertakes his/her decision exclusively on the basis of a forecast with an absolute conviction that this forecast is true. The 'certainty equivalence' therefore refers to the situation where the agent acts on the assumption that the probable proposition is true. This in turn eliminates the difference in the behaviour of the agent that might have emerged when undertaking a decision based on the expectation that something may happen as opposed to the expectation something will definitely (or certainly) happen.[16] In other words, by definition the agent rules out the possibility that his/her probable proposition may not be true, a consideration of which may make the agent alter his/her decision either by modifying it or by postponing it until obtaining further information. Thus with the assumption of 'certainty equivalence', the need for consideration of a possible change in the agent's behaviour is arrested. This in turn may reduce the obligation to reconsider our theoretical argument and its conclusion, but in the process it limits understanding of the way this market operates, thereby opening up the possibility of producing a policy which may become counter-productive, as has happened in the past. The problem with the replacement of information symmetry with information uncertainty, is that it changes the character of the operation of that market.

It is argued in this chapter that other than price, there are two additional factors that play a crucial role in the operation of this market, namely the credit standard and credit risk. The question is, why is this so? It is argued that when the payment remains uncertain, promises to pay alone cannot clear the loan market. Lenders introduce the credit standard in order to ensure that, should the borrowers default on loans, there remains some other means to enable lenders to recoup their loan capital, without which this market breaks down. The issue of credit risk principally arises here, owing to the fact that in the competitive atmosphere in which this market operates, lenders are not able, in all circumstances, to secure their loans by the credit standard. The credit risk therefore refers to that portion of the loan which is not secured by the credit standard, so that, should the borrower default on a loan, that is the portion of the loan that will not be recouped from the proceeds of the credit standard.[17] It is the variation in the credit standard implemented by the respective lenders which causes the variation in access of different groups of borrowers to the loan market. Now once our theoretical understanding of the nature of the operation of this market has been formulated, we are then in a position to investigate what went wrong with the policy of financial liberalization, and for that matter, with the policy of intervention that was adopted in the past.

In Chapter 4 we investigate the theoretical foundation on which financial liberalization rests. We then introduce the concept of the credit standard into this model to examine whether the same result can be obtained as the policy prescribes. Our analysis suggests that instead of bringing efficiency to the operation of this market, there is a good possibility that theoretically this policy can bring financial crisis. This means some form of intervention will be required in the operation of this market.

In Chapters 5 and 6, with this in mind, we investigate the types of intervention that have taken place in South Korea and India. We chose South Korea and India, as opposed to any other countries, for specific reasons. The level of intervention that has taken place in these two countries is roughly similar. The governments of both heavily intervened not only in the operation of the financial market, but also in their industrial and rural sectors. However, there is a subtle difference between India and South Korea, in the specificity of their intervention in the operation of the financial market. In India, while the emphasis was on providing cheaper credit to small enterprises and to the rural sector, in South Korea the emphasis was on providing credit to specific government-selected industries. The result of these interventions on the performance of the economy remained quite modest for India but robust for South Korea. In both cases, intervention in the operation of the financial sector made this sector fragile and in these two chapters, we examine the intervention in order to understand the factors that caused this fragility. This may allow governments of the respective countries, as well as those of other countries, to avoid such forms of intervention, with such adverse consequences, in the future.

In Chapter 7 we present the conclusion.

NOTES

1. For developed nations such as Australia, the UK, the USA and Japan on this issue see Basu (1986, 1989), Bolton (1972), BIE (1981), Campbell (1981), Caves and Uekusa (1976), Jappelli (1990), Johns *et al.* (1983), Juttner and Bird (1976), MITI (1983), Report of the President (1982), Storey (1982), Thomson and Leyden (1982), Wilson (1979). For the developing nations, for example India, see Bagchi (1992), Bardhan and Rudra (1978), Basu (1982, 1997), K. Basu (1983, 1984), Bhaduri (1973, 1977), Bhatt and Roe (1979), Ojha (1982), Rudra (1992) and Roth (1979). For Chile see Nisbet (1967), for Egypt see Eshag and Kamal (1967), for the Philippines see Griffin (1974). See also U. Tan Wai (1957), Bottomley (1964, 1965, 1975), Myrdal (1968). For an excellent survey of various nations see Little *et al.* (1987).
2. See Goodhart (1995) for further details on this issue. He also gives an excellent account of a series of 19th century crises. See also Fisher (1932), Hawtrey (1944), Sayers (1960a), Kindleberger (1989), Matthews (1954), Minsky (1977) and Calomiris and Mason (1997) on the above issue.
3. See Basu (1989) for further details on this issue.

4. See Basu (1997) for more on this issue.
5. Against these observations Robinson wrote (1931, p. 3), 'So long as the curing of the consequent unemployment remains imperfect, the gains of efficiency are worthless ... since the leisure is given not to those who wish to enjoy it, but to those who would prefer to be occupied.'
6. See Basu (1986) for further details on this issue.
7. Entitlement set refers to the individual's command over goods and services. This is defined as the set of all possible combinations of goods and services that an individual can legally obtain by using the resources of his/her endowment set (where resources includes both tangible assets, such as land, other assets, income, and intangibles such as knowledge and skill, labour power, or being a member of a particular community). See Sen (1981) and Osmani (1995) for more on this issue. Thus by enlargement of the entitlement set we mean an increase in the availability of a combination of goods and services as well as an increase in an individual's own endowment set, so that each individual will have a higher command over goods and services.
8. See Sayers (1960a) for further details. See also Hawtrey (1944) on the issue of credit controls.
9. For example, in the case of Australia, the New South Wales and Victorian state governments have established loan guarantee schemes since 1978. The Commonwealth Development Bank, prior to its privatization, used to be one of the major sources of providing long-term loans to small businesses for the purchase of plant and equipment (Johns *et al.*, 1983). In the UK, the government decided to stand as a direct guarantor for small businesses, anticipating that this would ease the capital availability problem. In addition, the government directly provided some financial help to small firms to purchase machinery, and also introduced a Business Start-up Scheme (Basu, 1986). In the USA, the Small Business Administration (a government-sponsored organization) also provided 70 percent guarantees for small businesses to ease their capital availability problems (Report of the President, 1982). Similarly, the Japanese government developed certain government-affiliated organizations to provide cheaper, as well as long-term, loans. They also provided loans in order to update the small manufacturing sector, so that small manufacturers could keep pace with modernization (MITI, 1983). See Basu (1986) for further details.
10. This is the general view expressed in the Campbell Committee's Report (1981); a similar view was also expressed earlier in the Bolton Committee's Report (1972). See also Smith (1776) who considered the detrimental impact of the ceiling in the context of usury.
11. See Krishnaswamy *et al.* (1987), Cho (1989) and Sen and Vaidya (1997) for further details on this issue.
12. See Krishnaswamy *et al.* (1987) and Little *et al.* (1987) on the above issue.
13. For the Latin American financial crisis see Diaz-Alejandro (1985). For a detailed account of bank failure see Goodhart (1995) and for the Australian financial crisis see Basu (1994). Furthermore, the recent financial crisis in Asia is another example of the failure of such a policy; see Miskin (1999), Arestis and Glickman (2002) and Basu (2002).
14. It is this argument that was put forward by Blinder and Stiglitz (1983) in order to explain how monetary policy works.
15. Of course, it would be extremely imprudent not to mention that Keynes himself was partly responsible for the development of the above framework and this is clear in his writing. As he wrote (1936, p. 24), 'By his [the entrepreneur's] expectation of proceeds I mean, therefore, that expectation of proceeds which if it were held with certainty, would lead to the same behaviour as does the bundle of vague and more various possibilities which actually makes up his state of expectation when he reaches his decision.' See Hart (1949) and Robinson (1980) for more on this issue.

16. See Hart (1949) for more on this issue. Even in the modern era, theoretical argument also proceeds by replacing uncertainty with the assumption of 'certainty equivalence'. For example, in the asymmetric information literature, the strategic interplays between agents are formulated by assuming agents are rational, and their prior probability distribution and their utility function are common knowledge (Brandenburger and Dekel, 1990). Alternatively as Milgrom and Roberts (1987, p. 184) write, 'the probability distribution over the particular private information of the various players could be common knowledge'. Essentially it amounts to redefining the game in such a way that each agent knows the probability distribution of the variable which is uncertain. Thus the game whose outcome is supposed to be uncertain has been transformed or re-arranged in such a manner that the absence of information is replaced with complete information about the probability distribution. See also Harshanyi (1967–68).

17. For a further explanation of credit standard and credit risk see Chapter 3.

2. A critical review of the literature on credit rationing

It has been noted for a long time that the allocation of credit is not guided by the price mechanism alone. In other words, banks not only use price but also use a non-price mechanism to ration credit. This form of behaviour by banks was noted by Keynes (1930, p. 365), as he wrote,

> There is, that is to say, in Great Britain an habitual system of rationing in the attitude of banks to borrowers – the amount lent to any individual being governed not solely by the security and the rate of interest offered, but also by reference to the borrower's purposes and his standing with the bank as a valuable or influential client.[1]

The question is, why is this so?

The literature on the theory of credit rationing is vast and the theoretical explanation does not follow from the issue that arises from Keynes' observation, but rather emerges from a debate that occurred during the 1950s in the USA in relation to how monetary policy works. This debate is known as the availability doctrine. The availability doctrine puts forward a view that even if it is found that investors (i.e. borrowers) are insensitive to changes in the interest rate, monetary policy still works owing to the fact that suppliers of credit are sensitive to changes in the interest rate. This is for the two following reasons. Firstly, they argue that the imperfections in the money market arising from the oligopolistic and monopolistic competitive structure and the varieties of government regulations, prevent interest rates from rising in the presence of an excess demand for loans. Secondly, they argue that for some peculiar reason, when the yield on private securities rises in relation to government securities, lenders do not switch from the latter to the former. The first argument identifies the exogenous factors, while the second identifies the endogenous factors, which cause bankers to ration credit in the presence of excess demand. The identification of these two factors as a possible explanation for bankers rationing credit, led to the development of two separate theoretical explanations. One is based on the argument that the ceiling on interest rates does not permit banks to offer a default risk-adjusted interest rate, and therefore banks deny loans to those who offer a higher default risk. The other is based on the argument that the borrowers' expected capacity to pay does not rise proportionately with the increase in the contractual payment and, as a result, beyond a certain level of interest rate or certain size of loan, banks deny loans to borrowers, as there is an increase in the risk of default.[2]

This chapter is divided into three sections. In the first section we will briefly investigate the availability doctrine in order to trace how these two contradictory theoretical explanations have emerged. In the second section we will investigate whether the exogenous factor, as theoretically presented, can provide a sufficient reason as to why banks ration credit to some borrowers. We then in the third section will investigate the validity of the argument, as suggested by the proponents of the other theoretical explanation, that the borrowers' expected capacity to pay does not rise proportionately with an increase in the interest rate, and as a result there is an increase in the default risk. This causes banks to introduce rationing.

2.1 THE AVAILABILITY DOCTRINE

By the late 1940s there was a growing uneasiness among economists in relation to how monetary policy works. Theoretically it is claimed that it works via investors' sensitivity to changes in the interest rate, which is thought to arise because a higher interest rate reduces the net return of an investment project. Therefore investors are likely to abstain from undertaking investment when the interest rate is high, which in turn will reduce the demand for loanable funds. In other words, higher interest rates will slow down economic activity. However, this claim was refuted by the Oxford price inquiry group, led by Wilson and Andrews (1951) in the late 1930s. This group conducted a survey to find out how sensitive businessmen are to changes in the interest rate. The survey reported that businessmen consider interest rate is a cost just like any other, and as long as the expected profit is high, they are not too concerned about the cost factor. Subsequently, White (1956 and 1958) and Grey and Brockie (1959) also empirically investigated this relationship. White found that investment at best is less sensitive to changes in the interest rate than theoretically claimed, while Grey and Brockie found that investment is not at all sensitive to changes in the interest rate.[3] In other words, the relationship between these two variables, interest rate and investment, is not as strong as that claimed by the theory.

This raises the question then as to how monetary policy does work. It was Roosa (1951), in the hearing of the Patman Committee, who put forward the view that even if it is found that borrowers are largely insensitive to changes in the interest rate, monetary policy still works via credit squeeze. This argument is centred on the notion that, at a given interest rate, the demand to hold government bonds will be relatively higher compared with other assets, if the interest rate is either increasing or has just increased, than if it remains stable. This is due to the combination of the three following factors: firstly, the imperfection in the money market does not permit the yield on other assets to adjust to compensate for the increased attractiveness of the government bonds; secondly, the irrational and conventional behaviour of the financial institutions means that portfolio decisions are not based wholly (or entirely) on yield comparisons, but rather are partly based on the reluctance to realize capital losses; and thirdly, uncertainty and expectations force economic agents (i.e. borrowers and lenders) to evaluate the economic future more cautiously (Tobin, 1953).

The availability doctrine argument rests on the assumption that the commercial banks' ability to extend loans at any given point in time is directly related to the availability of their reserves. Thus at any given point in time if the demand for loans exceeds the supply, there will be a tendency for the interest rate to rise. In this situation, if banks wish to meet the demand they have three options via which they can increase the supply of loans. They can raise the interest rate on time deposits, or borrow from the central bank, or sell government securities. The existence of a ceiling on time deposits in the 1950s known as the Q ceiling, rules out the first option.[4] Secondly, it is argued that banks do not wish to be seen to be in debt for long. This leaves them with only the third option, that is to sell government securities that they hold over and above the reserve requirements. It is argued by the proponents of the availability doctrine that the banks' willingness or unwillingness to sell government securities is largely influenced by the central bank's action. The central bank can influence this willingness or unwillingness by selling government securities or by lowering the price at which it will buy them. Either course of action will cause an increase in the yield of government securities, which discourages banks and other lending institutions from selling these securities to make provision for alternative loans and investments. According to the availability doctrine this discouragement principally arises due to the two following reasons. Firstly, if the banks as a group wish to sell these government securities in order to raise their available reserves, then they have to sell below the book value of these securities in order to induce other parties to buy them, which means they have to make some capital loss on the sale. Banks do not like to make this capital loss, even when their alternative assets offer a higher yield. This behaviour is referred to as the irrational behaviour of bankers. Secondly, the existence in the market of varieties of institutional rigidities (which include government regulations and oligopolistic competition), prevents the yield of these alternative assets from rising, relative to government securities. This makes the government securities more attractive compared with the alternative assets when the interest rate is rising. Therefore the argument is advanced that in this situation, lenders will ration credit to their private borrowers and some will be denied loans altogether. Thus the convention will keep the rate charged by the banks to their commercial borrowers from rising and the loan applications which would have been accepted previously will be denied. Hence the argument that, even if it is correct that the borrowers and spenders are unlikely to be deterred by a higher interest rate, monetary restriction is effective in curtailing spending.

While the imperfection argument convinced many participants of the hearing of the Patman Committee, the reluctance to accept a capital loss or, in other words, the irrational behaviour of the lenders, did not convince many. In fact, as Tobin (1953) pointed out, several executives of the insurance companies explicitly denied the claim made by proponents of the availability doctrine. According to these executives, such losses do not concern them if other assets offer a higher return. Samuelson also raised doubts about the relevance of this argument, as Tobin noted (1953).[5] The theoretical argument against this claim was put forward by Smith (1956). Smith not only holds a sceptical view about the availability doctrine, but also holds a similar view about the effectiveness of monetary policy alone to curtail expenditure. We will confine Smith's argument to that which is relevant to the availability doctrine.[6] While Smith does not dispute that the financial institutions' portfolio adjustments are sensitive to very small changes in the interest rate, he argues that these changes are also influenced by the maturity dates of the security. He argues that changes in the interest rate do cause a change in the price of the securities, but the magnitude of this change depends on their maturity date. For example, when the interest rate rises, short-term rates rise more than the long-term rates, but the price of the short-term securities falls less than that of the long-term securities.[7]

In this situation, according to Smith, one would expect that the institutions, such as those providing life insurance, which mainly hold long-term government securities, would be deterred from switching from government securities to loans and other securities, as opposed to banks which mainly hold short-term government securities. The switching of insurance companies, which are not subject to the same regulations as banks, from government securities to say corporate securities, will depend on whether the yield on the latter can compensate sufficiently for the cost of switching and for the additional risk. The cost of switching refers to the loss that will be incurred from the sale of government securities. Thus the switch depends on the interest rate differentials between government securities and corporate securities. If the borrowers or investors have an inelastic demand with respect to changes in the interest rate, then there is nothing to prevent these institutions from switching from government securities to corporate securities. Thus perhaps the only factor which prevents them from switching is that the investors are less inelastic than is claimed.

In the case of banks, to begin with Smith argues that when considering all other varieties of lending institutions operating in the lenders' market, even if banks have an oligopolistic power in their own market, this position disappears in the open market operation due to the presence of other lending institutions. This means banks' ability to curtail overall spending via rationing to their own borrowers is somewhat restricted. Furthermore, Smith (1956, p. 593) argues that, 'The process by which banks determine the volume of their loans and the terms on which the loans are made is one that is poorly understood.' According to Smith, most banks in their dealings with customers are in an oligopolistic and, often, a monopolistic position, which in turn gives them considerable power to discriminate between their borrowers. However this power varies from one group of borrowers to another. For example, it is considerably reduced when dealing with large established borrowers who have a regional or national reputation with alternative avenues to raise funds, including the power to utilize open market facilities. Furthermore, most businesses and households have an established connection with one bank only. The volume of loans that a bank can advance depends on the interest rate charged and also on the minimum credit standard[8] that it imposes on the borrowers. As a result, a bank is faced with a number of different demand curves, each revealing the amount it can lend at different interest rates, with a different curve for each set of credit standards that it might set. This is the peculiar feature of a bank's demand curve.

Given this analysis, Smith then argues that customers are their bread and butter, and customer relationships are very important. Furthermore loans are more remunerative than investments.[9] Now if the demand for credit increases, banks may ration credit initially by tightening up the credit standard without making much change to the interest rate. But they like to meet the 'legitimate' demand of their customers and in order to do so they will sell their secondary reserves.[10] As banks mainly hold short-term government securities, they are likely to incur only a very small loss in the event of selling their secondary reserves, which could easily be compensated for by a small rise in the interest rate on loans. This therefore suggests that at least on theoretical grounds there is no reason why banks will not accept a capital loss on government securities in order to make funds available for private borrowers, especially when the latter have an interest inelastic demand curve.

Following Smith's paper, Kareken (1957) and Scott (1957a, b) make an attempt to eliminate the irrationality element from the argument of the availability doctrine. Kareken's main contribution to this literature is that he attempts to separate the rationing phenomenon that arises as a result of changes in monetary policy from the one that arises owing to the imperfection in the money market; the latter phenomenon is independent of the former. His argument centres on the notion that banks hold secondary reserves as a safeguard against the loss of demand deposits. An increase in the yield of government securities causes a fall in the market value of their secondary reserves, and therefore these reserves become inadequate. This induces commercial banks to increase their holding of government securities in order to maintain an adequate safeguard. Thus changes in the yield of government securities cause a change in the asset preferences, which in turn causes a change in the structure of the loanable fund market, resulting in a lower availability of funds for private borrowers. This therefore suggests that the effectiveness of monetary policy relies on the process of credit rationing, which is independent of the rationing that arises from the imperfections that prevail in the money market. In relation to the imperfect market, Kareken argues that bank loan rates are not competitively determined, but rather are determined administratively. Furthermore, owing to the presence of oligopolistic or monopolistic competition, the price or yield remains inflexible. As a result there remain a great deal of non-price forms of rationing.

But Kareken recognizes the problem in his own argument, which is that the process requires a switch from private securities to government securities. To hold this preference in favour of government securities one needs to assume that the yield on private securities will remain unaltered, while the yield on government securities will increase. This means that the yield on private securities must fall relative to that on government securities. But we have been told that private borrowers have a relatively interest inelastic demand curve. This means when the yield on government securities increases, the yield on private securities must also increase in order to attract loanable funds. If the borrowers have an interest inelastic demand curve, then there is nothing to restrain private borrowers from offering a higher yield. In this situation the question which remains to be answered is why bank funds, instead of moving to the private market, move into government securities. Kareken recognizes that unless a logical reason can be provided for this peculiar behaviour of the lenders, the irrationality element cannot be removed from the argument. Accordingly, he suggests that there is a need for modification of the new theory in relation to the argument concerning credit rationing.

Scott's (1957a, b) thesis is centred on the notion that an increase in the yield of the government securities causes a change in the structure of risk in the investors' portfolios. He argues that investors generally divide their portfolios between government securities and private securities. Both types of securities bear a certain amount of risk. Risk in government securities principally arises from the possibility of change in their market value, should their investors decide to sell them prior to their maturity date. Risk in private securities, on the other hand, is not only subject to market risk, but also to credit risk. Market risk is the risk that arises from the possibility of changes in the market value of securities, whether government or private. Credit risk, in the absence of any further explanation, is an alternative expression for default risk.[11] That private securities carry both forms of risk suggests that they in general offer a higher risk than government securities. It is assumed that risk and return represent a linear relationship, otherwise no one would hold private securities. As the investor's portfolio is composed of both types of securities, this suggests that there must be a limit on the maximum amount of risk that each investor is prepared to take. The combination of these two securities that makes up a portfolio will of course differ between individuals, and be determined by their taste and preference for risk. For example, a risk taker may have more private securities in his/her portfolio than will a risk averter.

Given this analysis, Scott argues that when the yield on government securities increases, it increases the market risk of the secondary reserves (composed of government securities) owing to changes in their market value. This may induce investors to switch from government securities to private securities. But the switch involves, first, the making of a capital loss on the government securities, with the expectation of higher earnings from the private securities and the possibility that this expectation may not be realized due to credit risk. Thus the risk will be increased by two factors should investors decide to switch in the event of changes in monetary policy. Accordingly, Scott argues that such a switch to private securities means in fact undertaking a greater risk than that which will be required in the absence of any policy change. But in the absence of such a switch, the risk of the existing portfolio combination will even exceed the limit of the risk that any individual investor is prepared to take, owing to the fall in the market value of the secondary reserves. Consequently, investors take measures commensurate with the maximum risk they are prepared to take. In other words, they will buy more government securities as opposed to private securities. This action in turn causes a reduction in the availability of funds for private borrowers. But this still does not provide a satisfactory answer to the question raised by Smith, which is, when borrowers have an inelastic demand with respect to changes in the interest rate, why does the yield on private securities not rise sufficiently to compensate for the additional risk that is required to induce bankers to switch from government securities to private securities?

The availability doctrine's inability to solve this latter issue led to the development of two contradictory theoretical explanations of credit rationing. One proceeded along the line of the imperfection argument, i.e. government regulations, such as a ceiling on the interest rate itself, prevent banks from offering default risk-adjusted interest rates, and as a result banks ration credit to some borrowers. The other proceeded to search for an answer to the question, why does the yield on private securities not rise sufficiently to compensate for the loss that will occur should a bank's loan portfolio switch in favour of private securities?

Interestingly, neither of the subsequent theoretical developments takes note of the important issue of the bankers' behaviour that was pointed out by Smith. This consists of their insistence on a minimum credit standard that the borrower must meet,[12] against which they advance loans, variability in the credit standard for different groups of borrowers, and the different interest rates that different groups of borrowers have to pay, some of which issues were also raised by Keynes (1930). Nor does the subsequent literature take note of (or address) Kareken's argument that the loan rates are administratively determined rather than competitively determined, or for that matter Scott's point regarding the credit risk which he introduces into his argument in order to differentiate the risk between private securities and government securities. But before we address these issues, in the following two sections we will investigate two theoretical explanations that follow from this doctrine.

2.2 THE CEILING ON INTEREST RATES AS A POSSIBLE EXPLANATION FOR BANKS REFUSING LOANS TO SOME BORROWERS

The success of Keynesian activism in fighting the Great Depression in western countries, and of the Marshall Plan in reconstructing the war-damaged economies in the West, as well as the success of Soviet industrialization during the 1930s, constituted a tacit intellectual consensus that government has an important role to play in shaping and re-shaping the economy. This was the predominant view until the 1960s and was referred to as the Keynesian perspective. During this period, governments of developed as well as developing countries intervened in the financial system in various ways. One of these was an attempt to provide cheaper credit facilities to lower socio-economic groups (which included small businesses and small farms). Accordingly, a ceiling on the interest rate was imposed in various nations, and in addition to this, in the case of developing countries, varieties of specialized banks were developed in order to assist the lower socio-economic groups' access to the loan market.

Several decades of experience suggest that these government-sponsored agencies have, in the case of developing nations, in fact benefited large industrial houses, and large landowning and middle-class farmers who could have obtained loans at commercial rates from their local banks without much difficulty. Similarly, in developed countries, it has also been observed that in the case of these varieties of loan guarantee schemes, a ceiling on interest rates has not improved the access of these groups of borrowers to the banks' loan market. In other words, these intervention policies have been unable to improve the access of these groups of borrowers to the loan market in any appreciable manner to justify their continuation. In fact, the view that has been expressed is similar to one expressed in the availability doctrine. Here, on the issue of why the interest rate on loans does not rise sufficiently to compensate for the additional risk that may be involved in switching from government securities to private securities, the argument lends more support to the explanation of the imperfect functioning of the market, arising from its oligopolistic and monopolistic nature and from government regulations. In this case it was similarly argued that the ceiling on interest rates does not permit banks to accommodate the additional risk that is involved in offering loans to these groups of borrowers. Thus the regulations add to the imperfection, thereby reducing the access of those for whom the regulations were implemented. For example, the Bolton Committee (1972) which investigated small business problems in the UK and the Campbell Committee (1981) which investigated the Australian financial market, both drew a similar conclusion, that is, that the ceiling on interest rates further heightens imperfections in the financial market. Both argue that the provision of subsidized loans or special facilities will not save the small business sector. Bolton suggested a freer financial system would improve the flow of finance, while Campbell thought it would remove the distortion from the supply side.[13]

A theoretical analysis of this failure has so far been provided by McKinnon (1973) and Shaw (1973). Although their arguments are presented for developing nations, they are equally applicable to developed nations. These two authors argue that the ceiling on interest rates not only distorts the functioning of the credit market, but helps large borrowers to obtain loans at a subsidized rate. They argue that the ceiling on interest rates which was initially imposed on banks and which was based on the idea that smaller and poorer borrowers would receive loans at a cheaper rate, soon becomes counter-productive. That is, the ceiling itself prevents smaller and poorer borrowers from entering into the orbit of the organized money market because it does not permit banks to incorporate into the calculation of the interest rate the additional risk and administrative costs that are involved in each small loan and, as a result, the ceiling itself reduces banks' incentive to lend to those borrowers who offer higher risk.[14] Consequently, banks advance loans only to those who offer lower risk and better security, which implies that only the rich industrial class and wealthy landlords receive loans at a cheaper rate (than would have been possible without the ceiling), leaving the small and poor borrowers to seek loans from the unorganized credit market. Thus they argue that the removal of the ceiling on interest rates would allow banks to incorporate extra loadings that are associated with the additional risk and the extra transaction costs that are involved in small loans. This in turn would eliminate the banks' disincentive to loan to small and poor borrowers.

As the central argument rests on the default risk, it is necessary to examine whether this risk can be put forward as the reason for the persistence of high interest rates. The combined effect of the default risk and the excess demand phenomenon (or the monopoly power) should increase interest rates to a high level, and thus it is necessary to examine whether these higher rates will compensate for the resulting additional risk. It is to this problem we now turn.

With respect to any loan that is advanced by a lender, whether it is advanced by banks or by private money lenders, there remains some risk and uncertainty in relation to whether that loan will be repaid. We make a distinction between risk and uncertainty: risk is calculable to its precise magnitude, while it is not possible to calculate uncertainty. Risk and uncertainty arise in relation to payments because there is a time difference between the advancement and the repayment of loans, and during this interlude the borrower's situation may alter and consequently borrowers may default on loans. As the above authors (e.g. McKinnon, Shaw, Mellor and Bottomley) have not taken into account the issue of uncertainty, for the moment we will ignore the problems that are associated with it, and will proceed with a discussion of the risk analysis. However, the issue of uncertainty will be taken up in the following chapter. Recognition of the risk factor implies that every lender, whether a banker or private moneylender, must calculate the probability of default risk of his/her borrowers. This calculation is necessary because, on the one hand, it allows the lender to decide whether to advance a loan, and on the other, it is required to determine the effective interest rate.

Suppose a lender advances a loan amounting to L_0 with the anticipation that the borrower at some future date will return L_1 amount where $L_1 > L_0$.[15] On the basis of this promise from the borrower, the lender advances L_0 amount of loan.

$$L_1 > L_0 \text{ because of the interest rate } r,$$

$$\text{i.e. } L_1 = (1 + r)L_0$$

where r is determined by

$$r = \frac{L_1 - L_0}{L_0}$$

This is the interest rate the lender expects to receive, but it is in the absence of default risk, in other words, when the default risk is zero. In the presence of default risk the actual interest rate is referred to as the effective interest rate that a lender would receive and it may deviate from the quoted interest rate, since there remains a possibility that a portion of the loan will not be repaid. Therefore, prior to advancing the loan the lender must calculate the probability of the occurrence of this fraction and incorporate it into the calculation of the interest rate. Suppose there remains the probability π that a fraction of the loan, i.e. q, may not be repaid. In other words, πq may not be repaid. This suggests that the actual amount a lender will receive, say L^*, may deviate from L_1

$$\text{i.e., } L_0 \overset{>}{\underset{<}{-}} L^* \leq L_1.$$

Thus we can write,

$$L^* = (1 + r)(1 - \pi q)L_0 \tag{2.1}$$

Suppose the risk-free interest rate in the urban area is i, then the risk-adjusted interest rate in the rural area is as follows:

$$i = \frac{(1 + r)(1 - \pi q)L_0 - L_0}{L_0} \tag{2.2}$$

and from the above equation we get,

$$i = r(1 - \pi q) - \pi q \tag{2.3}$$

Thus we get $\qquad r = \dfrac{i + \pi q}{1 - \pi q} \tag{2.4}$

Now if $\pi q > 0$, i.e. positive, in the absence of risk adjustment $r < i$, or in other words, the effective rate of interest will be less than the interest rate that was agreed to by the borrowers and lenders. It is for this reason one needs to incorporate the risk factor into the calculation of the interest rate, as indicated in the above equation.

Given the above analysis, let us examine whether it is possible for village moneylenders to enjoy a high interest rate, e.g., 360 or 200 percent as noted by Nisbet (1967) and McKinnon (1973) respectively within the framework of default risk.

Consider a hypothetical example: for the sake of simplicity, assume a poor farmer in the rural area has a 100 percent probability (i.e. $\pi = 1$) of not returning a fraction of the loan. Assume at equilibrium, the interest rate (i.e. in the absence of default risk) in the organized sector is 10 percent, i.e. $i = 0.1$. We know from Nisbet and McKinnon that $r = 3.6$ or 2.0 respectively. Manipulating equation (2.4) to find the value of πq and inserting these values in the following equation, we get,

$$\pi q = \frac{r - i}{1 + r} = 76 \text{ percent or } 63.33 \text{ percent respectively.} \qquad (2.5)$$

The above calculation highlights an interesting fact: if the interest rate is 360 or 200 percent as observed by many authors (e.g. Griffin, 1974; Bottomley, 1975; Nisbet, 1967) and if it is due to the high default risk as, for example, is suggested by Bottomley (1964, 1975) and Mellor (1968), then it is immaterial whether the interest rate (i.e. the default risk-adjusted interest rate) is 100 or 200 percent, since a major portion of the loan would not be repaid. Furthermore, we assume $\pi = 1$ for demonstrative purposes; this means as π moves from 1 to 0, q will not only approach 100 but will move beyond it, which is not feasible. In this situation, it is not only reasonable to argue that the removal of the ceiling is unlikely to attract commercial banks to extend their loan facilities to the rural borrowers, but it is equally unlikely that a rural lender can benefit from such a high interest rate.

The above argument therefore rules out both the default risk and the combination of default risk and the excess demand phenomenon, and for that matter also the combined impact of default risk and the monopoly power (whatever that may mean), as an explanation for the high level of interest rates in rural areas. Therefore from the above analysis we cannot deduce why the banking sector in general remains reluctant to extend credit facilities to the rural poor or what is the cause of high interest rates.[16]

Although the above analysis was carried out with reference to the rural market, it is equally applicable to small businesses. This is simply because the default risk-adjusted interest rate means that in the event of default, a fraction of the loan, i.e. q, will not be repaid. The proponents of this view did not recognize a serious problem that remains with the concept of default risk-adjusted interest rate. To begin with, this rate neither prevents borrowers from default nor protects banks in the event of default. Furthermore, the higher the adjustment, the higher the value of q, which means it is the lender who is more likely to lose in the event of default, as shown above. Thus the lack of provision for the default risk-adjusted interest rate cannot be the reason why banks in general abstain from offering loans to lower socio-economic groups.[17]

This leaves the only reason for which the ceiling on interest rates prevents banks from offering loans to lower socio-economic groups is the fact that the ceiling does not permit banks to incorporate the additional transaction costs that are involved in advancing smaller units of loans. Therefore a ceiling on interest rates reduces banks' expected profitability. This then may be a reason, which is independent of other endogenous reasons, why they may abstain from offering loans to lower socio-economic groups.

Now this leads us to investigate the other explanation for credit rationing, which also emerges from the availability doctrine, to see whether this theory can shed some light on this matter.

2.3 CAPACITY TO PAY DOES NOT RISE IN PROPORTION TO THE RISE IN THE CONTRACTUAL PAYMENT: AN EXPLANATION OF CREDIT RATIONING

This theoretical explanation of credit rationing attempts to provide an endogenous reason for the rationing of credit by banks. Such rationing may even arise in the absence of exogenous impediments. This theoretical development of credit rationing was initiated by Hodgman (1960), but it originated from the unsatisfactory reason that was presented by the availability doctrine for banks not switching from government securities to private securities when the latter offered a higher yield compared with the former. Scott (1957a, b) attempted to answer this question by arguing that such a switch increases the risk of the loan portfolio. But he was unable to explain why the yield on private securities does not rise sufficiently to compensate for the additional risk. Hodgman recognized that to address the above question one needs to develop a theory of credit rationing that arises independently of exogenous factors. Accordingly he wrote (1960, p. 259),

> My purpose is to provide a more general explanation for credit rationing which does not rely upon oligopolistic market structure or legal maxima to the interest rate, which is consistent with rational behaviour along lines of economic self-interest, and which is permanent rather than temporary in its effect for so long as the general credit situation which occasions it lasts.

Hodgman argued that the yield and risk aspects of an investment are systematically interrelated within a specific limit when considering individual borrowers. Thus, with a given credit rating, the risk of loss is an increasing function of the size of the loan, while the expected gain or loss is an increasing function of the borrowers' promises to pay. A borrower's credit rating sets the upper limit of the expected value of the pay-off. This upper limit itself implies that as the size of the loan increases, the expected gain from an additional unit of loan will not compensate for the expected loss that arises from the additional unit of loan. In other words, beyond a certain size of loan, the value of the expected loss will exceed the value of the expected gain from an additional unit of loan. Therefore bankers will ration credit to borrowers no matter how high the interest rate they offer. His analysis is based on the assumption that the capacity to pay is determined by the borrower's existing assets, and therefore it is independent of the size of the loan. This means (or gives the impression that) his rationing was only applicable to the non-investment borrowing groups. Subsequently, Chase (1961) extended Hodgman's analysis to the case of investors. Chase argued that as the size of the loan increases it will also increase the size of the investment, and therefore it will increase the capacity to pay. However, as the size of the investment is not monotonically related to the rate of return, it is implied that beyond a certain point the rate of return will increase at a declining rate as the size of the investment gets larger, and will reach an optimality point and then fall. This declining rate of return with a increasing size of investment increases the default risk as the loan size gets larger, thereby causing the ratio of the expected gain to the expected loss to approach zero. Bankers will ration credit to borrowers because they know that beyond the point of zero the expected loss will exceed the expected gain. This explains why the supply of loans to any individual becomes perfectly interest inelastic or even becomes a backward-bending, upward-sloping curve, beyond a certain size of loan.[18]

Freimer and Gordon (1965) consider this form of rationing to be weak. They argue that in the presence of excess demand bankers may not increase the interest rate, since it may not only reduce the demand for loans but also increase the default risk. As the higher risk of default reduces banks' expected profitability, bankers may prefer to negotiate loans within a limit at a lower interest rate. Thus their argument is centred on the notion that the extension of a loan beyond a certain size, even at an existing rate, will increase the default risk to a level where the expected loss from the additional loan will exceed the expected gain.

Thus the essence of the argument of these authors is that no matter how high the interest rate that is offered, it cannot compensate for the risk of default. These arguments were further advanced by Jaffee and Modigliani (1969), who argued that there exist risk differentials among borrowers, although they may engage in similar projects with an equal size of operation. Thus, in the presence of excess demand, when a borrower offers a higher interest rate than that offered by other borrowers from a similar group, that borrower will be classified as a high risk borrower. Therefore such a borrower will either be denied a loan or will receive less than that demanded. In other words, an increase in the interest rate will be accompanied by loans of a smaller size.

The above theoretical explanation of credit rationing that followed from Hodgman to Jaffee and Modigliani, is based on the assumption that higher interest rates or larger loans increase the default risk, thereby reducing bankers' expected profitability and thus banks introduce a non-price rationing device. This default risk, according to them, arises from the fact that capacity to repay does not rise proportionately with a rise in the contractual payment, which emanates as a result of an increase either in the interest rate or in the size of the loan. This result was derived from the well-known theoretical argument that while the rates of return on an investment project increase as the size of the investment increases, beyond a certain point, the return increases at a declining rate, reaches an optimality point, then falls. In other words, this is based on the second-order condition of the differential equation, which is that the rate of return and the size of the investment are not monotonically related. But the contractual payment is an increasing function of the interest rate or size of the loan. This means the contractual payment must converge to the rate of return of an investment project before reaching its optimality point. Since investment ceases at the optimality point, the issue of rationing does not arise. This leads to the question, why do borrowers or investors not cease to borrow at the convergence point or before it, since at that point investors' net return will be zero?[19] In particular, when borrowers know that in the event of default, as Jaffee and Modigliani (1969) point out, the lender becomes the owner of the firm, why does a borrower wilfully invite such an outcome? This leaves theoreticians with an uneasy question to resolve. In other words, there is still a need to show why default risk increases, given the situation described above. Without this explanation the literature loses much of its relevance.

Subsequently, Jaffee and Russell (1976) and Stiglitz and Weiss (1981) attempted to explain why higher interest rates increase the default risk. Their argument essentially rests on the notion that while their capacity to pay may be known to the bankers from the borrowers' expected return from their investment project, what is not known to the bankers is the borrowers' risk, due to the presence of asymmetric information. This risk is the one that arises from the individual's attitude towards risk, and is said to be the function of the individual's pecuniary situation. Accordingly, Jaffee and Russell (1976) argue that an increase in the interest rate may adversely affect the amalgam of good and bad borrowers, while Stiglitz and Weiss (1981), in addition to that, argue that a higher interest rate induces firms to undertake more risky projects. These two effects are known as the adverse selection and the incentive effects. The adverse selection effect suggests that those who have a preconceived notion that their probability to repay the loan is low, are more likely to remain in the pool of loan applications at a higher interest rate. The incentive effect, on the other hand, suggests that as the higher interest rate reduces the expected net return of projects which succeed, this may induce borrowers or firms to switch from a so-called low risk to a high risk project, where the probability of success is low, and where the return will be high in the event of success. Thus the essence of the argument is that although capacity to pay may be known from the investment project, what is not recognized is that changes in the interest rate may bring about the above two effects, thereby altering the risk structure of the loan portfolio, and thus introducing the possibility of adversely affecting the borrowers' capacity to pay. In other words, changes in the interest rate may adversely affect the quality of loans, thereby reducing banks' expected profitability. Thus in the presence of excess demand a rational profit-maximizing banker, instead of raising the interest rate, introduces a non-price form of rationing.[20]

As the central argument is based on two key assumptions, we will confine our examination to these assumptions, and to whether they are adequate to establish why rationing emerges in the operation of this market.

The adverse selection effect states that for those who have a preconceived notion that their probability of repaying the loan is low, a higher interest rate will not be a disincentive for them to borrow. This means as the interest rate increases, low risk borrowers will leave the pool of loan applicants, thereby leaving only the risky borrowers. Thus the interest rate itself acts as a screening device to identify the risky borrowers, and therefore they will be rationed credit by banks. But the problem with this assumption is that these borrowers' riskiness is determined by the fact that they have a preconceived notion that their probability to repay the loan is low. This means they are unlikely to be concerned about the level of interest rate, and thus they are likely to remain in the pool of loan applicants when the interest rate is low. Thus the higher interest rate may be able to identify high risk borrowers, but no mechanism is left to identify borrowers according to risk, at a lower interest rate. Therefore it is quite possible that these high risk borrowers will receive loans when the interest rate is low. This means we should expect a higher default rate when the interest rate is low. Furthermore, as far as the rationing is concerned, as the less risky borrowers leave the pool of loan applications, only the risky borrowers remain to be rationed.[21] This leaves the debate wide open as to whether bankers do not raise the interest rate because of the borrowers' interest elastic demand for loans, or because of their fear that it may increase the riskiness of the loans. Freimer and Gordon (1965, p. 416) point out that offering loans at a higher interest rate may not generate much demand, 'while it may encourage borrowers to negotiate loans within this limit at a lower interest rate'. This leaves us to examine Stiglitz and Weiss's second assumption.

Their second assumption states that as the higher interest rate reduces investors' net return for the projects that succeed, this may induce borrowers or firms to switch from a low risk project to a high risk project where the probability of success is low, and where the return will be high in the event of success. But they overlook two important factors that must be considered when making the decision to switch between projects following changes in the interest rate: (a) there is a cost associated with selection and switching between projects and (b) the possibility of an adverse impact from the crowding out effect. The issue of the switching cost arises owing to the fact that investment expenditure is largely irreversible. That is, these are mostly sunk costs and therefore cannot be recovered. Therefore, if a firm wishes to switch from a low return to a high return project, which may involve switching from one industry to another industry, or from a cheaper product to an expensive product, it must take into consideration the net loss that will accrue as a result of the sunk costs from the old project. This is because a firm's capital (i.e. plant and equipment), marketing techniques and advertising techniques are all to some extent specific to that project. These therefore, in their present form, will be of little or no use for other projects or other industries, so are sunk costs. In principle, a firm should be able to sell its plant and equipment to any other firm which is involved in that specific project within the industry. However, as the value of plant and equipment will be about the same for all firms within that industry, it is unlikely that one firm will gain much, if anything at all, from selling it.

Furthermore, in the event of changes in the interest rate, if a firm considers that its current project's net return is not sufficient in comparison with the high interest rate, then this view should be shared by other firms operating in that industry. Therefore, all firms from that industry would have the same inducement effect. That is, they all would like to switch from low return to high return projects. In these circumstances, firms either will have no buyers for their plant and equipment, or will be forced to sell well below the current market value in order to induce other firms to buy. In either case, this suggests that a switch between projects involves a substantial loss to a firm, due to the irreversible costs.[22] It follows that once we consider the incorporation of the switching cost as well as the selection cost, the firm's net expected rate of return may not rise sufficiently to induce it to switch from a low to a high return project, even when the new project offers a higher expected rate of return.

On the other hand, if we assume that switching between projects does not necessarily imply switching from one industry to another, the sunk costs may be small but we cannot ignore the adverse impact of the crowding out effect. That is, if all firms within the industry decide to switch from low return projects to high return projects (i.e. from low return products to high return products), then this movement will in turn not only reduce the return of the so-called high return projects, but also increase the risk of the projects, because of the greater competition that emerges as a result of the greater supply of firms. This is equally applicable in the case of switching between industries.

The above argument suggests that switching between projects in the event of changes in the interest rate is possible provided we assume capital is malleable[23] (since malleable capital has properties that eliminate the additional costs involved in switching) and there exists an unlimited demand in the market to absorb all additional firms without adversely affecting the price of the product. From the above it follows that if the switching between projects involves satisfying the above two conditions, then it is unlikely that existing firms which are already committed to projects will be in a position to make any possible additional gain by switching from those with low returns to projects with higher returns. Thus the possibility of receiving a lower expected net return remains high in the event of high interest rates, irrespective of the choice of projects, i.e. whether they choose to continue with the old project or switch to a new one. This leaves firms who are yet to commit to any project, and the question here is whether a higher interest rate will induce these firms to switch from a low risk to a high risk project. But the problem is, as interest rates oscillate virtually from month to month, the process of production from its initial state to completion in general takes longer, during which time the variation in interest rate will cause the expected net return of a project to oscillate also. Consequently, it becomes impossible for the investor to calculate the expected net return of the project with any precision, in the absence of knowledge of the future oscillation of the interest rates, until the completion of the production process. The problem is that the level of interest rate is only one of many factors that play a role in the decision to invest in any project, and therefore it may be too demanding to suggest that an investor's decision to invest in any project will be influenced by the level of interest rate alone.

Furthermore, the higher expected rate of return and the risk are not the only two criteria on the basis of which entrepreneurs select their projects. They are also influenced by their knowledge and familiarity with that project. In most cases, entrepreneurs do not have sufficient information in relation to all projects available to them, leading them to select the project they know best, and this is to some extent irrespective of the level of the interest rate. This therefore suggests that there remain limitations in the selection of a project even after changes in the interest rate, due either to unfamiliarity with other available projects or to the additional cost that will be involved in switching between projects.

Thus it is difficult to establish the proposition that the increase in the interest rate will bring about the possibility of a large scale incentive effect, thereby introducing the possibility of adversely affecting borrowers' capacity to pay. Thus a careful examination of the two assumptions devised by Stiglitz and Weiss to explain why bankers, in the presence of excess demand, do not raise the interest rate, suggests that neither provides a convincing reason for the possible adverse effect of interest rate increases on borrowers' capacity to pay.[24] This perhaps gives the impression that banks do not raise the interest rate in the presence of excess demand, owing to the fact that higher rates may reduce the borrowers' net return, and therefore cause the demand for loans to fall. But as the rationing even occurs at the existing rate, as shown by Freimer and Gordon (1965), this suggests that the only reason for which the rationing may emerge depends on there being a difference in the evaluation of the capacity to pay by lenders and borrowers, as suggested by Hodgman (1962). This leads to the question as to how and why the difference between lenders and borrowers emerges in their evaluation of borrowers' capacity to pay. In order to answer this question we need to examine the issue of the credit standard referred to in Smith's paper (1956) and the credit risk in Scott's paper (1957a, b), but neither of these authors defines what he means by it and why it is important. A similar issue was also raised by Keynes (1930) and by Viner in a letter to Keynes, but neither provides an explanation.

It will be argued subsequently that it is the borrowers' differing entitlement set and the recognition of this set by the lenders, referred to as the credit standard, which determines the lenders' assessment of the borrowers' capability (or capacity) to repay the loan. It is the variation in this capability, as estimated by the lenders, which causes the variation in their access to the loan market. It is to this problem we turn now.

NOTES

1. A similar observation was also made by Viner (1937). In fact Viner, in a letter to Keynes in 1946, expressed his astonishment about economists' lag in recognizing the role of rationing, as he writes, 'The lag of economists in recognizing the role of rationing (or availability) of credit as a regulator has always astonished me' (Bloomfield, 1992, p. 2076). Hawtrey (1944) also made a similar observation.
2. This literature is reviewed by Baltensperger (1978), who covers its development from the 1960s to 1970s, and Jaffee and Stiglitz (1990), who cover the period from the 1960s to the birth of the modern theory. But neither of the above studies discusses how this literature has emerged nor its historical significance, and nor do they review the literature that has developed from the failure of government regulations. As a result, from this point of view, the review of this literature is somewhat incomplete.
3. See also Sundarajan and Thakur (1980), Roe (1982) and Khatkhate (1988) whose examination reconfirms earlier findings. For earlier works on this issue see Shackle (1946) and Lutz (1945).

4. In fact, Friedman (1971) subsequently argued that the Q regulation was one of the prime reasons for the development of the Euro-dollar market.
5. See also Chase (1960) on this issue.
6. Participants in a symposium on these controversial issues related to monetary policy were Harris (1960), Angell (1960), Fellner (1960), Hansen (1960), Roosa (1960), Samuelson (1960), Smith (1960), Thomas (1960), Tobin (1960) and Weintrub (1960). See also Sayers (1960b), Fei (1960), Minsky (1957) and Modigliani (1963) on these issues.
7. See also Scitovsky (1940) on this issue, who argues that when the current interest rates increase, investors expect future interest rates over their planning horizon to rise but by less than the rise in current rates.
8. For the definition of credit standard see Chapter 3.
9. Investment here refers to banks' investment portfolios. A bank's asset portfolio generally comprises a loan portfolio and an investment portfolio. The investment portfolio is composed mainly of government securities. These government securities, which banks have to hold under the rule of the required reserve ratio, are over and above the minimum cash reserves they hold in order to meet depositors' demands, and are referred to as secondary reserves.
10. For the definition of secondary reserves see note 9.
11. This is an issue that will be taken up in Chapter 3.
12. See also Sayers (1949), Wilson (1954), Lindbeck (1962) and Galbraith (1963) on the above issue.
13. See Basu (1989) for further details.
14. Similarly, Mellor (1968) and Bottomley (1964, 1965, 1975) argue that interest rates are high in the rural area due to high default risk.
15. Payments in this loan market are one-off, that is, for example in the case of agriculture, borrowers borrow prior to the harvest and repay the principal plus the interest just after the harvest, and therefore it is not valid to calculate these interest rates in the usual per unit time. See Basu (1997) for more on this issue. See also Rudra (1992).
16. See Basu (1997) for more on this issue.
17. In fact it will be argued in Chapter 3 that it is not possible to calculate the precise magnitude of the default risk in advance. See Basu (1989, 1994 and 1997) on this issue. This does not necessarily mean that a banker does not take note of the past loan performance prior to advancing a loan to a borrower. In fact a borrower's credit rating plays an important role in a lender's decision whether or not to advance a loan.
18. See also Miller (1962), who develops the rationale for credit rationing in terms of lenders' taste, where he uses the expected utility hypothesis as a declining function of the interest rate.
19. This is an issue that was raised by Ryder (1962). Hodgman's (1962) reply to this question was that the rationing phenomenon principally emerges due to the difference in the subjective evaluation of the investment project by the two interested parties.
20. See also Bester (1985, 1995), Diamond (1984), Riley (1987), Gale (1989), Gertler (1992), Gertler and Gilchrist (1994), Jaffee and Stiglitz (1990), Keeton (1979), Myers and Majluf (1984), Besanco and Thakor (1987), Bhattacharya and Thakor (1993), Calomiris and Hubbard (1990), Bernanke and Gertler (1989) and Williamson (1986) on this line of work.
21. Riley (1987, p. 226) points out that, 'the extent of rationing implied by S-W model is not likely to be very important empirically'.
22. See Pindyck (1991) for more details on this issue.
23. See Garegnani (1978) who argues that at any given instant available physical capital

cannot be fluid, so it cannot take an appropriate form to adjust to the new level of interest rates.

24. This perhaps may explain why policy makers did not pay attention to this literature despite its enormity, when making the decision to liberalize the financial market, and instead relied more heavily on the argument of exogenous factors as causing the rationing phenomenon to emerge.

3. The theory of credit rationing revisited

3.1 INTRODUCTION

The issue of credit rationing principally arises when two individuals are prepared to pay the price, and one receives the loan, while the other is either denied the loan altogether or receives less than he or she demanded. The question is, why is this so? In other words, why do two individuals have different degrees of access to the loan market?

It is argued in this chapter that bankers operate in the presence of uncertainty, and as a result cannot calculate in advance the precise magnitude of the probability of borrowers returning the loan (i.e. principal plus interest rate). In other words, they cannot calculate the precise magnitude of default risk on an a priori basis. Consequently, bankers employ credit standards as an alternative means to recoup the loan, should the borrower's project fail. The credit standard (which includes some form of security or collateral) therefore is an attempt to insure banks' loan capital against uncertain outcomes. When loan applicants do not meet banks' credit standards, their applications will generally be rejected. In fact, most failed credit applicants are those who do not meet banks' credit standards. This is because the banker knows that in the event of a borrower's failure to maintain the repayment rate, it is the bank that has to bear the major cost. Thus these borrowers are not profitable in the bank's eyes.

However, the credit standard that banks set is not determined entirely by bankers' wish to avoid risk and uncertainty, but rather is determined by the competitive atmosphere in which they operate. As a result, bankers are often unable to set a credit standard that can fully secure their loan capital. In this situation, they have to take some credit risk.

Credit risk refers to that risk which arises when the loan capital is not fully secured by the credit standard. This means, should there be a default on a loan, the portion of the loan which is not secured by the credit standard will not be recouped from the proceeds of the credit standard. The level of credit risk that a bank is willing to take varies from one borrowing group to another, and is determined by the borrowers' own bargaining position in the lenders' market (which in turn is determined by their own standing with the banking authority and the purpose for which they seek loans). It is the variation in the credit risk which causes different borrowers to meet different levels of credit standard, which in turn causes different borrowers to have different levels of access to the loan market.

The literature on credit rationing that follows from Hodgman attempts to explain the rationing phenomenon that often emerges from shortages in the banks' cash reserves,[1] however it is not clear what the role of the credit standard is in such explanations. For example, in Stiglitz and Weiss's model, where collateral explicitly enters into the loan contract, the explanation of the credit rationing phenomenon exclusively relies on the adverse selection and incentive effects. This raises the question, what is the role of collateral as a determinant of the credit standard in such a model? After all, by definition the above two effects only arise when borrowers are less likely to lose in the event of project failure. Collateral entering into the loan contract means borrowers have something to lose in the event of project failure, unless we assume that only the assets that are purchased with the help of the loan capital are used as collateral in the loan contract. In this form, an increase in the collateral requirements, instead of reducing the lender's risk, will increase it and this was recognized by Stiglitz and Weiss. This might have left them with the option to use the borrower's attitude towards risk, which is normally non-identifiable,[2] as a possible explanation for rationing. But importantly what is perhaps overlooked on this occasion is that such a form of collateral requirement at best can be described as an alternative expression for equity finance, and therefore loses the attributes that are necessary to fulfil the task of the credit standard.[3]

This chapter is divided into three sections. In the first section, we investigate why banks introduce the credit standard as a means of ensuring the return of their loan capital, an issue which has not received any significant attention in the existing literature. In the second section, we investigate why the credit standard alone cannot protect the banks' loan capital, and the measure that banks attempt to take, over and above the credit standard, in order to protect this capital. In the third section, we investigate why access to the loan market differs between two individuals.

3.2 THE CREDIT STANDARD

Loan contracts between bankers and borrowers take place on the basis of future rates of return, where both borrowers and bankers believe that borrowers' future rates of return (assuming the borrower is an investor) will be sufficient to pay back the principal plus interest. The formation of this belief is based on past and current rates of return from similar projects. This assumes that borrowers intend to invest in a project whose rate of return can be assessed from past and current experience. The above procedures suggest that loan contracts are based on investors' or borrowers' expected future stream of earnings. It is this expected future stream of earnings that allows borrowers to promise to pay the principal plus the interest in the future. Borrowers derive this expectation largely from their current ability and willingness to pay. However, their current ability to pay is derived from their current stream of earnings, and it is not certain that their future stream of earnings will be sufficient to maintain this ability. There is thus a possibility that both borrowers' ability and willingness to pay may change in the future.

As the investor's or borrower's income or rate of return on an investment is directly related to the quantity of goods or services that can be sold at a given price, or with a change in price assuming costs are minimized,[4] changes in demand will directly affect his/her revenue, and thus the rate of return.

Neither borrowers nor bankers have full knowledge of the future direction of demand as they do not have knowledge of the future direction of those factors that influence demand, such as the price of the commodity, the price of substitutes, the price of other commodities, the consumers' real income, the distribution of income and consumers' taste and preferences.[5] Furthermore, they also do not have much control over these variables.[6]

This means both parties enter into a contractual agreement on the basis of a belief that the borrower's future rate of return from the project for which the loan was advanced will be sufficient to pay back the principal plus the interest. The issue of belief, or for that matter expectation, principally arises here, as neither the borrower nor the lender knows with certainty what the future outcome will be. In other words, the project has more than one probable outcome. That is, the project's future rate of return may be greater than the contractual repayment rate, may be equal to it, or may fall below it. None of these outcomes is known with a precise magnitude, either to the borrower or to the lender in advance. The lender will be concerned with whether the project's future rate of return will fall below the contractual repayment rate. This problem principally arises here as neither the borrower nor the lender knows the future demand price of the project for which the loan was issued. Hence the contractual agreement occurs on the basis of information about the project's current and/or past performance. However, the problem is that one cannot totally rely on such an expectation, as this means elimination of the distinction between past and future, so that the information asymmetry can be eliminated. Elimination of this information asymmetry is only possible if one implicitly assumes that time is moving backwards and forwards, which in turn allows us to predict the future demand on the basis of past information about those variables that have played a role in the project's outcome. But the problem is that time only moves forwards, and therefore it is perfectly possible that the project's past performance may not repeat itself.[7] This problem remains with the risk analysis that so often is used for projection purposes.[8]

The risk analysis, which primarily involves estimating the probability and magnitude of changes in those variables that are supposed to determine the outcome of the project, relies on past and current information. For example, let us assume

$$E(x) = f[E(p_x), E(y)] \qquad (3.1)$$

and they are represented by a linear function where $E(x)$ is the expected quantity demand for commodity x, $E(p_x)$ is the expected price of the commodity x and $E(y)$ is the consumer's expected income. Changes in the value of variables such as $E(P_x)$ or $E(y)$ will cause a change in the demand for commodity x, assuming x is a normal good.

$E(x)$, $E(P_x)$ and $E(y)$ are weighted averages of the different values of x, p_x and y respectively, with weights given by each of their respective probabilities derived from past and current information. Alternatively, we can write,

$$E(x) = \sum_{i=1}^{n} x_i \pi(x_i)$$

$$E(p_x) = \sum_{i=1}^{n} p_{x_i} \theta(p_{x_i})$$

and

$$E(y) = \sum_{i=1}^{n} y_i \phi(Y_i)$$

The problem is that these independent variables may move beyond the estimated values, which in turn will cause the actual demand to deviate from its estimated value. If such movements are small we can calculate their approximate effect on demand assuming parameter values, i.e.

$$\frac{\partial x}{\partial p_x} \text{ and } \frac{\partial x}{\partial y}$$

remain constant for all values of p_x and y respectively. That is,

$$Ed_x \approx \frac{\partial x}{\partial p_x} E(dp_x) + \frac{\partial x}{\partial y} E(dy) \tag{3.2}$$

The adequacy of this approximation is a much debated issue as Modigliani and Miller (1958, p. 252) indicated, 'yet few would maintain that this approximation is adequate'. For the sake of simplicity it is assumed that this approximation permits prediction of the trend in demand.

However, if the changes in the independent variables are large, this causes a change in the parameter values, and thus it is not possible to estimate their effect on the outcome of x. Alternatively an inaccurate estimate will be given of the outcome of x. Thus when changes in the independent variables are large it is not possible to derive the expected outcome of x, that is,

$$E(dx) \neq E\left(\frac{\partial x}{\partial p_x} dp_x\right) + E\left(\frac{\partial x}{\partial y} dy\right) \tag{3.3}$$

unless

$$\frac{\partial x}{\partial p_x} \text{ and } p_x, \frac{\partial x}{\partial y}$$

and y are independent of each other. If, for example,

$$\frac{\partial x}{\partial p_x}$$

and dp_x are independent of each other, it is possible to derive mathematical expected values. However, it is unlikely that they are independent. Furthermore, these variables have been used as discrete variables for illustration but, in reality, they are more likely to be continuous, leading to further difficulties in evaluating the expected value of outcomes for commodity x. Furthermore, the above approximate estimation follows from the fact that we have pre-assigned probability values for each respective independent variable, derived from the past distribution of probabilities, but it is unlikely that the future distribution of probability will in practice fall within the boundary of their pre-assigned values.

This suggests that in the absence of future values of the independent variables and their probability distribution, it is unlikely that we shall be able to predict the future outcome of any investment with any accuracy. The above estimation illustrates the problem of estimating the future demand. This suggests that the risk analysis suffers from two weaknesses which are irremovable and they are as follows: (a) if the future movement of those variables falls outside the observed variation, then there will be a difference between the projection and its *ex post* result, (b) if the probability values themselves change or their frequency changes, then the expected value that has been calculated with the previous probability value will be liable to error.[9] This therefore suggests that in the absence of factual content, calculations will be liable to misleading information (or expectation). This means that the introduction of time brings uncertainty in relation to the future rates of return. Uncertainty principally arises here because the future position of the variables that have in the past produced a favourable outcome for the project, is not known and there remains a possibility that their position or value may change, which in turn may break the continuity.

The above analysis therefore suggests that in the presence of incomplete information, risk analysis will not eliminate an uncertain outcome. This is because uncertainty mainly arises due to the lack of factual information, while risk analysis relies on factual information. Therefore, the latter is an inadequate tool to address the former.[10] We can conclude from the above analysis, that in the absence of knowledge in relation to the future position of those variables that are likely to influence demand, we cannot estimate the precise magnitude of the future demand. As the return is derived from the difference between the revenue and the cost of production, in the absence of knowledge in relation to the future demand it is not possible to estimate the future revenue with accuracy. This prevents the possibility of estimating in advance the precise magnitude of future rates of return.

This means that the current evaluation of the prospective yield of an investment project does not necessarily reveal the true objective value of the capital asset.[11] Entrepreneurs are involved in decision-making concerning an uncertain future, about which there is neither any real objective basis on which to evaluate possible outcomes nor any means of insuring against undesirable outcomes.[12]

This means there is no objective basis on which to calculate with accuracy in advance the probability of either repayment or default. Therefore, the possibility of over- or under-estimation of risk will always remain.[13]

The above analysis therefore suggests that a rational banker who is attempting to maximize his/her own expected utility function cannot make a decision whether or not to advance a loan solely on the basis of such a calculation. This is because, when the borrower's project outcome remains uncertain, there is no certainty that the actual interest rate, referred to as the effective interest rate that a borrower will pay, will not deviate from the quoted interest rate. Bankers cannot with precision calculate in advance the margin of this possible deviation, and therefore the effective interest rate will remain indeterminate.

Let us illustrate this problem with the help of the formulation that we devised in the second section of Chapter 2, with a minor modification. In the case of the former, the explanation was based on a one-off payment, while in this case it is based on an nth period payment. Suppose a lender advances a loan of L_0 at period t_0 and the amount the lender expects to receive at the end of the period t_n is L_n^e where $L_n^e > L_0$. Needless to say, unless this condition is met lenders are unlikely to advance L_0. $L_n^e > L_0$ because of the bank's interest rate r, i.e. $L_n^e = (1 + r)^n L_0$. Bankers expect to receive L_n^e in the absence of uncertainty. However, in the presence of uncertainty a lender will receive L_n^* where $L_n^* \leq L_n^e$. The possibility of this deviation between L_n^e and L_n^* mainly arises because the value of L_n^* depends on the borrowers' projects, the outcome of which is not known, while the value of L_n^e is determined by the bank's interest rate r. Bankers are mainly concerned if $L_n^* < L_n^e$. Alternatively, we can say they are concerned that there remains a possibility that a fraction of the loan may not be repaid.

Suppose q is that fraction of the loan which may not be repaid, where

$0 \leq q \leq 1$, and π is the probability that q will occur, where $0 \leq \pi \leq 1$. In these circumstances, bankers are required to know the value of πq in order to determine the effective interest rate defined as R, which in turn will determine the size of L_n^*,

$$\text{i.e.} \quad L_n^* = [(1 + r)(1 - \pi q)]^n L_0 \quad (3.4)$$

Now we know that the effective interest is

$$R = \left(\frac{L_n^*}{L_0}\right)^{\frac{1}{n}} - 1 \quad (3.5)$$

Thus we get the following result,

$$R = r(1 - \pi q) - \pi q \quad (3.6)$$

The value of πq depends upon the borrowers' projects' outcomes, which are not known to the bankers. As a result they cannot estimate the effective rate of interest, i.e. R remains indeterminate. All they know is, if $q > 0$ then $R < r$. Bankers advance loans on the condition that $R = r$, which only holds when $\pi q = 0$. Now as explained, in the presence of uncertainty it is not possible to determine the value of πq. In this situation, the only avenue left for bankers is to undertake measures that eliminate or minimize (or neutralize) the adverse impact of πq. In other words, the impact of πq from the bankers' point of view on loan returns will either be zero or close to zero. This is only possible if banks can secure the entire principal by collateral or some form of security. That is, whatever the value of q turns out to be in the future, bankers will sell part of, or the entire, collateral to eliminate the adverse impact of q, i.e. $q = 0$. If the competitive atmosphere does not permit bankers to ensure that $q = 0$, then they will make an effort to ensure that at least q's impact remains close to zero. That is, bankers will take all measures to ensure that R is either equal or close to r.

The above argument therefore suggests that bankers are required to take a measure to ensure that should the borrowers default on a loan, they have alternative means of honouring their debt obligation. Accordingly, bankers ask for collateral as an alternative means of repaying the loan should a borrower's project fail, referred to as the credit standard.

It is for this reason that we find wealth plays such an important role in determining borrowers' access to the loan market, and it suggests that, in this market, the interest rate alone does not determine demand. We need to distinguish between a borrower's desire for a loan and the demand for loans.[14] The demand for loans not only depends on the interest rate, but the recognition of such demand by the banker depends on whether the borrower can meet the bank's credit standard. Any borrower who wishes to borrow, but who cannot meet the bank's credit standard requirements will not receive a loan.[15]

3.3   CREDIT RISK

Theoretically, any item which has a relatively stable value and a ready market can be used as collateral, but the acceptance of such items varies from banks to private lenders. While some private lenders would readily accept jewellery or even kitchen utensils as collateral, these items are not recognized by banks, which commonly take houses and land as collateral, against which they issue loans.[16] Banks do not accept small items as collateral due to the cost of storage facilities; also they may not be interested in engaging in such small loans as it may not allow them to achieve economies of scale because of the high transaction costs involved. In other words, the cost of advancing small loans may outweigh the benefit. This may be why we find poor borrowers, despite their low default rate in general, only have access to the loan market that is controlled by private moneylenders and the poorest borrowers have even been denied access to this market (Basu, 1997). The collateral that is accepted by the bank or by the private lender is in general subject to fluctuation as the state of the economy changes, and as the individual's own financial circumstances change.

We will confine our argument here to the case of banks. Banks are only concerned about the reduction in the value of collateral, and they know that it is neither possible to predict such a reduction nor its precise magnitude in the absence of knowledge in relation to the future state of the economy and the future state of the borrower's own financial circumstances. Consequently, bankers take a very cautious approach to these estimations, and they accept an asset as collateral on the basis of its current market value and attempt to lend a little less than this value. They do not attempt to estimate the future value of the house, for example, and then offer loans accordingly. This is mainly because they know that there remains uncertainty in relation to the estimation of the asset's future value. In other words, the estimated future value of an asset may be greater or smaller than its actual market value. The above argument suggests that there is a possibility that the collateral may not be able to secure the principal. Thus in the event of a worse outcome for the project, there is the possibility that the borrower will fail to maintain his/her promises. Furthermore, he/she may not even be in a position to return the entire principal to the lender.

This problem is further complicated by other factors, such as when collateral may be a disincentive to borrow. Securing the entire loan (i.e. principal plus interest) by collateral means that the borrower now has to bear the burden of the entire uncertainty, while the profits that accrue in these circumstances will be shared between both the borrower and the lender.

Banks confront this problem particularly when they deal with large borrowers or large clients. Large borrowers, due to their large asset backing and good track record, not only have access to banks, but also have access to other parts of the capital market. In this situation, a large borrower (i.e. an investor) will be inclined to raise finance by issuing shares rather than by resorting to loans, assuming the state of the equity market is such that it readily offers these facilities. Furthermore, due to the competitive structure in which these lending institutions operate, it is unlikely that lenders in all cases can secure the entire portion of the principal by collateral. This suggests that part of the loan remains unsecured, especially the interest rate payment. In this situation, bankers are required to take an additional measure over and above the credit standard they set. This measure is particularly important when the credit standard cannot secure the loan.

The portion of the loan that is not secured by the credit standard and would not be recouped from the sale of the collateral should the borrower default, is referred to as the credit risk. Credit risk therefore refers to that portion of the loan which is exposed to the possibility of default, i.e. the difference between the size of the loan and the market value of the asset against which the loan was advanced. Thus there is a need for bankers to make a provision in advance against this credit risk, which provision attempts to ensure that, should the borrower default on the loan, the bank does not have to bear the cost of non-performing loans. Normally banks incorporate in advance the cost of such loans into the calculation of the interest rate. This cost is referred to as the risk premium, and often provides a windfall profit to banks.

In our opinion much of the misunderstanding in the literature on credit rationing arises here as the subtle distinction that exists between the credit risk and default risk is not acknowledged, and this problem primarily arises because the authors of this literature have not investigated why banks introduce credit standard requirements. Instead, they continue to use default risk as an alternative expression for credit risk.[17] By default risk we mean that there is a probability that the borrower may default on a loan. Thus if this probability value is known in advance, it is possible to calculate in advance what fraction of the loan will not be repaid should the borrower default. But if this probability value is not known, then a lender cannot calculate in advance what fraction of the loan will not be returned. In other words, in this situation there remains a possibility that should the borrower default on his/her loan, the lender may lose an amount of the loan capital, ranging from a fraction above zero to the entire amount. Of course a lender cannot operate with this range of possible loan losses, and the lender needs to know in advance the fraction of the loan that will not be paid should the borrower default. This fraction is only known in advance once we introduce the credit standard requirement, which in turn allows us to determine what fraction of the loan is not secured. The fraction of the loan that is not secured by the credit standard will not be returned should the borrower default on the loan, and this fraction is referred to as the credit risk. Now once this fraction is known it is possible to calculate the approximate level of credit risk on a loan. This in turn allows lenders to calculate the expected loss, which they then compare with the expected gain, in order to decide whether or not to advance a loan or an additional unit of loan.

The issue of rationing in the presence of excess demand has really evolved with the question of why banks remain reluctant to take on higher credit risk. In other words, the credit rationing literature addresses the question of why, when it seems necessary, for example during periods of development or for that matter during periods of excess demand, rational profit-maximizing bankers remain unwilling to extend a larger quantity of loans by taking a greater credit risk and compensating themselves by offering a credit risk-adjusted interest rate. From Hodgman to Stiglitz and Weiss, there have been attempts to provide an explanation for this particular behaviour of bankers.

The problem with the credit risk-adjusted interest rate arises not only from the fact that, in reality, it can save the bank only if a few borrowers default on loans; it also arises, at a fundamental level, from the fact that this interest rate suffers from serious inherent shortcomings, which

cannot be overcome. The adjustment procedure involves the multiplica-
tion of the credit risk by the number of possible defaulters, which determines the total value of the loss should the precise number of assigned
borrowers default on loans, then dividing this value by the number of
possible non-defaulters. This determines the risk premium, which is
incorporated into calculation of the interest rate. So we can write:

$$d = \frac{\{nL(1+i+z)-[(1+i+z)L(n-x)+xc]\}}{L(n-x)} \Big/ t \qquad (3.7)$$

where

d is the risk premium
n is the number of loans advanced by the bank
L is the average size of the loan advanced by the bank
x is the number of possible defaults
c is the collateral
i is the depositor rate that banks promise to pay
z is the administrative cost per unit of raising and advancing loans
     expressed as a percentage of the size of the loan, and
t is the repayment period.

Thus we can write:

$$R = (i + z)(1 + d) \qquad (3.8)$$

where R is the risk-adjusted interest rate that banks charge on loans.

The above equation highlights that the value of d depends upon the
size of x and the difference between L and c. The problem is, the higher
the number of x with a larger difference between L and c, the higher the
value of d will be, and this in turn will raise the interest rate to a level
which itself will increase the possibility of default. For example,
suppose $n = 10$, $L = \$100$, $x = 2$, with the probability that the 2 borrow-
ers will default being 1, $c = \$90$, $i = 10$ percent i.e. 0.1, $z = 0.2$ percent
i.e. 0.002 and $t = 1$. Given these values, from the above equation we get
$d = 0.0505$. This suggests that when the loan capital carries 18.33
percent credit risk,[18] in this situation if the assigned 2 borrowers default
on their loans, then for every dollar that is advanced with a promise to
pay the interest rate, \$0.0505 will not be returned. If we reduce the value
of c from \$90 to \$80 the credit risk increases from 18.33 percent to 27.4

percent, and the value of d increases from 0.0505 to 0.0755. Given the equilibrium rate of interest, i.e. $(i + z) = 0.102$, i.e. 10.2 percent, this suggests that in both of our examples, if the 2 borrowers default on their loans, then the banks will be able neither to recover their administrative cost nor to meet the depositors' rate. Furthermore, as we increase the credit risk, the total loss from each loan gets larger, other things being equal. In each of these respective cases, bankers then are quite likely to incorporate this loss into the calculation of the interest rate, which is referred to as the risk-adjusted interest rate. In other words, when $d = 0.0505$, $R = 0.107151$, i.e. 10.7 percent, and when $d = 0.0755$, $R = 0.109701$, i.e. around 11 percent. This numerical example suggests that if we increase the credit risk and offer loans accordingly by adjusting risk into the calculation of the interest rate, it will increase the interest rate, which in turn may increase the number of possible defaulters. In other words, the risk-adjusted interest rate may cause the actual value of x to deviate from its estimated value, an argument that was put forward by the early authors of the credit rationing literature to explain why banks ration credit in the presence of excess demand. The limitation on the credit risk-adjusted interest rate principally arises here because the credit risk is inversely related to the credit standard. In other words, the higher the credit risk, the lower the credit standard will be.

The above scenario can be explained with the aid of a simple equation.

$$\text{Suppose } L = F(cp, c, cr, a \ldots p) \tag{3.9}$$

where

cp is the contractual payment which is determined by the interest rate (R) and the size of the loan (L)
c is the collateral
cr is the credit risk
   .
   .
p is the expected return on an investment project.

As cr and c are dependent on cp, if cp, cr and c are major factors (where banks try to control cr and c) we might perhaps expect a non-linear relationship between L and cp.

$$cr = g(cp) \qquad (3.10)$$

$$c = j(cr) \qquad (3.11)$$

Then

$$L = h(cp) \qquad (3.12)$$

Where h includes the effects of g and j. The above equation suggests that due to the presence of an interdependent relationship, if cp increases either as a result of an increase in the interest rate, as in Hodgman (1960) or due to the rise in the size of loan, as in Freimer and Gordon (1965), it will cause cr to rise, given the size of c. In this situation, banks will raise c in order to protect their loan capital, should borrowers default on their loans. As a large number of borrowers may not be able to meet their banks' higher collateral requirements, they will either be denied loans or will receive loans of a lesser size than that demanded, as suggested by Jaffee and Modigliani (1969), thus forming the 'fringe of unsatisfied borrowers' referred to by Keynes (1930). Otherwise it will adversely affect the quality of loans as suggested by Stiglitz and Weiss (1981).

The above analysis suggests that if the interest rate increases, or with a given interest rate borrowers ask for a larger loan, banks will ask for collateral of a higher value. In other words, higher interest rates or higher contractual payments will cause banks to raise their credit standards, and if the borrowers are unable to meet these higher credit standards, they will either be denied loans or will receive less than that demanded. Borrowers' inability to meet higher credit standards implies that in the banks' estimation, their capability to pay does not rise proportionately with the rise in the contractual payment, and as a result banks ration credit.

Banks insist on borrowers meeting higher credit standards when the interest rate rises, because it not only increases the credit risk but they know that the credit risk-adjusted interest rate itself further exposes banks' loan capital to credit risk. For example, when c = \$80, $(i + z)$ = 10.2 percent and L = \$100, 27.4 percent of the banks' loan capital is exposed to credit risk, and in this situation if a bank decides to offer the credit risk-adjusted interest rate which is 11 percent, given the value of c and L, the credit risk increases to 28.1 percent. This suggests that it is an inadequate method of adjustment. More importantly banks know that the credit risk-adjusted interest rate in reality can save a bank's loan capital only if a small fraction of the borrowers default on loans, and assuming there is a small difference between L and c. But the problem is that the difference between L and c depends on the competitive structure in which the lending institutions operate, while the value of x has to be decided in the absence of information about the future. In other words, whatever the value banks decide to assign to x, there remains always the possibility that its actual value may exceed its expected value. This problem is further complicated by the fact that the difference between L and c depends on the actual value of c realized at the time borrowers default on loans, which depends in turn on the state of the economy and the state of the defaulters' financial circumstances.

The above argument therefore may suggest that a rational profit-maximizing banker will always try to avoid taking any credit risk whenever possible. But this alone does not explain why two individuals' access to the loan market differs, as it only tells us why rational profit-maximizing bankers do not like to take a greater credit risk than is necessary. It is to this problem we turn now.

3.4 DIFFERENTIAL ACCESS TO THE LOAN MARKET

The level of credit risk that banks take does not entirely reflect their taste and preference for risk and uncertainty, but rather depends on the competitive structure in which they operate. The competitive structure normally refers to the level of competition, whose intensity purely depends on the number of players operating in the market, i.e. in this case how many banks and NBFI are operating in this market. The assumption here is that the higher the number of players, the greater the competition among these institutions to attract a larger number of depositors and borrowers. In short, these institutions will fiercely compete with each other either to retain or to extend their share of the market. In this situation, it is correctly claimed, a well-functioning stock market can increase the intensity of this competition. In the process, it is claimed, the borrowers' access to the loan market will be improved. We are only concerned here with the borrowers.

But the competitive structure has another aspect, which is not entirely determined by the number of lending institutions (which include all NBFI) that operate in the loan market. Rather it is determined by the rate of return on loans that lenders expect from different borrowing groups.

It is the latter factor which causes a variation in the level of competition that an individual lender or bank faces from its rivals, when they are competing for different groups of borrowers in the capital market. We argue that most of the results of competitive policies are derived by either ignoring this factor which causes a change in the structure of competition, or at best by assuming that the sheer number of players can eliminate the variation in the level of competition. It is not realized that this variation in the level of competition for different groups of borrowers which purely arises from the fact that different groups of borrowers offer different levels of expected profitability, in general cannot be overcome merely by increasing the number of lending institutions.

The variation in the level of competition principally emerges from the fact that different groups of borrowers with their different size of operation and asset backing, offer different levels of expected rates of return on loans. The demand for borrowers who offer higher than expected rates of return compared with others, will be high in the loan market. This higher demand in turn provides a choice to these borrowers. That is, they can either borrow from banks, or else can raise finance via NBFI, or can raise finance by issuing equity in the stock market. These choices suggest that those borrowers who offer higher than expected rates of return on loans are less dependent on banks as the only alternative source of raising funds. It is this range of options that is open to borrowers which forces banks to compete with the other parts of the capital market, when wanting to lend to those who offer higher than expected rates of return. We argue that, as a result, banks have little choice other than to make concessions to their credit standard requirements, in order to capture this end of the market. This means, as the borrowers' ability to offer higher than expected rates of return shrinks following their decreasing size of operation and asset backing, so too do borrowers' choices in raising funds from alternative sources, resulting in lower competition between banks for such borrowers, but this also causes the competition between banks and the other parts of the capital market to decline. In turn, this segregates the loan market.

Consequently, banks are not required to make any undue concessions to their credit standard requirements when operating at the other end of the market, i.e. with the pool of smaller borrowers as loan applicants. An important point to note here is that the competition that a bank faces not only depends on how many banks and other lending institutions are operating in the loan market, but also on the expected rates of return and assets that an individual borrower can offer. Accordingly, competition between banks and other lending institutions varies from one group of borrowers to another. Thus, when competition is high, banks are required to relax their credit standards in order to attract borrowers, and when competition is low banks are not required to take such action. It is for this reason that we observe that different borrowing groups have to meet different credit standards, which in turn causes a variation in the borrowers' access to the loan market. In other words, while some loans carry a high credit risk, others may carry zero credit risk.

The borrower's or firm's size of operation and its asset backing play an important role in the formation of expectations in relation to whether the firm's rate of return will be high or low. This is because the borrower's or firm's size of operation in relation to the total size of the market and in relation to its competitors' size, has an important bearing on determining the firm's power in the market. This in turn may not only influence the firm's own rate of return but also influence the probability of achieving such a rate of return. The importance of the size of operation mainly arises from the fact that variations in its size represent different rates of return with a different probability of achieving such rates of return.

The above analysis is based on two assumptions: (a) the greater the scale of operation, the lower the unit cost of production which arises from economies of scale. Thus firms in the same industry do not represent identical cost curves; (b) the greater the market share, the stronger the power to determine the market price. For the firm with a smaller size of operation, these two factors not only increase the possibility of reducing per unit profit margins but also reduce the possibility of obtaining lower rates of return per unit of investment. In contrast, a firm with a greater market share has a greater possibility of obtaining a higher rate of return, with a lower possibility of vulnerability compared with its smaller counterparts, where any changes in the economy are assumed to be due either to adverse shocks, to changes in the aggregate supply in relation to demand, or to changes in the demand condition. This implies that a firm's probability of success or failure and its expected return may represent a non-linear relationship within the industry.

All other things being equal, in general, the possibility of deviation from the firm's expected rate of profitability mainly arises for two reasons, one associated with the competitive atmosphere in which it operates, and the other arising from possible fluctuations in the macro-economic variables, e.g. in the aggregate demand. In either situation, it is argued below that the deviation from the expected rate of profitability is more likely to adversely affect the smaller firms than their larger counterparts.

One possible deviation from the expected value in a competitive atmosphere mainly arises because of the fact that all firms aggressively compete with each other in order to increase their share of the market. Thus for a given size of the market, an increase in the share by one firm has to be compensated for by a loss of share by another firm. An important point to note here is that whether a firm or group of firms is either able or unable to increase its share, this form of competition introduces a possible scenario where the aggregate supply of a commodity or commodities can exceed the demand. This is because, if a firm wants to increase its share of the market it has to increase its output beyond its own market requirements. Now if all firms produce according to the needs of their own market, a decision by a few firms to increase their share beyond their own market requirements can lead to a situation where supply exceeds demand.

The above analysis therefore suggests that this competition itself is likely to adversely affect some firms' profitability in relation to others, and often can adversely affect all firms within one industry if no one firm is able to improve its relative position in the market. However, the adverse impact of competition is likely to be borne more heavily by smaller firms than by their larger counterparts not only because of their smaller size of operation, but also, more importantly, because of the fact that they have limited alternative means of subsidizing the loss that may arise as a result of this deviation. Thus the competitive atmosphere within itself creates a possibility of deviation from the expected rates of return which does not flow from possible fluctuations in the aggregate demand (or aggregate effective demand).[19]

The other possibility of deviation that arises as a result of possible fluctuations in aggregate demand, is also more likely to have a greater adverse impact on smaller and medium sized firms. This therefore suggests that the size of operation in relation to the size of the total market itself presents a greater (for smaller firms) or lesser (for larger firms) likelihood of an adverse consequence, which will remain, irrespective of the type of industry with which a firm is affiliated.

Industry affiliation may simply heighten or lower the possibility of an adverse consequence in relation to a similar sized firm operating in another industry.

It is important to note that in the presence of uncertainty, the above analysis leaves the lending institutions with an alternative option, which is to use the firm's size of operation in order to form an opinion in relation to it's expected rate of profitability and its possible vulnerability, that arises from either the competitive atmosphere in which it operates and/or from possible fluctuations in the aggregate demand and from its own asset backing. This in turn contributes to the lending institutions forming an opinion in relation to the expected return on loans that they advance to any firm. Therefore, the lending institutions' expectations that accrue from the firm's size of operation and its asset backing, cause a variation in the level of competition within the financial market for clients. The demand for clients about whom these lending institutions, including banks, have already formed a lower expectation in relation to the profitability of the loan, will be low and vice versa. This in turn causes a variation in the level of competition between the lending institutions, and often this competition, especially between banks and the other parts of the capital market, even ceases. This in turn allows banks to set different credit standards for different groups of borrowers. In the case of extremely poor borrowers, banks even do not recognize the assets they can offer as collateral, and as a result they cannot meet banks' minimum credit standards, and therefore these borrowers resort to the unorganized credit market. For example, in the case of small and medium sized businesses, banks are often the only remaining avenue for them to raise external finance apart from friends and relatives, while in the case of large firms, banks are not the only providers of external funds. Furthermore, in the case of large firms, their larger size of operation with their greater asset backing allows them to demand larger loans, which in turn reduce the banks' administrative (or transaction) costs, compared with the firms' smaller counterparts. The combined impact of this lower administrative cost with the lower probability of default, increases banks' expected profitability to a much higher level than that which they expect from small loans. This therefore suggests that, if there is a necessity for banks not only to relax their credit standards but also to offer concessionary rates in order to attract large clients, they will have the incentive to do so. Furthermore, the existence of alternative sources of loans allows these borrowers to enjoy a bargaining power when dealing with banks, a situation which banks do not face when dealing with their other clients. As a result, we observe that as the borrowers' reliance on banks as their only alternative source of raising funds falls, so too does the cost of their debt.[20]

The above argument therefore suggests that the variation in the individual borrower's access to the loan market principally arises from the fact that different borrowing groups have to meet different credit standard requirements, set according to the expected rates of return that each individual borrowing group offers. The borrowing group that offers lower expected rates of return compared with their larger counterparts will have to meet a higher credit standard than the group that offers higher expected rates of return.

Thus it is the variation in the credit standard which explains why two individuals' access to the loan market differ.

3.5   CONCLUSION

The analysis that has been presented in this chapter suggests that if we introduce the concepts of credit standard and credit risk into the analysis of why banks may ration credit, this not only allows us to remove the confusion that remains in the literature, but also allows us to understand why access to the loan market differs between two individuals.

As the loan market operates in the presence of uncertainty, bankers introduce the credit standard as an alternative means of determining the borrowers' capacity to pay. This is a necessary step that a bank or, for that matter, any lender has to take in order to secure the loan capital against an unforeseen default possibility. The credit standard principally comprises collateral or some form of security which banks take as a mortgage, the value of which is equivalent to the value of the loan capital. In this situation, if a borrower demands a bigger loan, whose value exceeds the bank's credit standard requirements, either by offering a higher interest rate, as in Hodgman, or at an existing rate, as in Freimer and Gordon, the bank then has to either raise the credit standard requirements or deny the loan to that borrower. This is because an increase in the size of a loan at either the existing rate or a higher rate will increase the contractual payment. This means the credit standard that has been set previously in accordance with the interest rate and the size of the principal, is no longer sufficient to protect the loan capital (i.e. principal plus interest). In other words, the contractual payment will exceed the value of the security, which means a fraction of the loan now becomes unsecured, and this fraction will not be recovered from the proceeds of the credit standard. The portion of the loan that is not secured by the credit standard is referred to as the credit risk.

The credit rationing literature's simple argument is that bankers do not wish to take more credit risk than is necessary. This is because, other things being equal, although an increase in the size of a loan will increase the investor's expected capacity to pay owing to an increase in the size of the investment, this does not necessarily imply that the investor's actual capacity to pay will rise. Consequently, with a given credit standard this will cause a rise in the credit risk. Therefore, bankers either are required to raise the credit standard or reduce the size of the loan in order to bring back the credit risk to its previous position. Similarly, if the interest rate increases as a result of excess demand for loans, with a given credit standard requirement, banks will offer a loan, the size of which is less than that demanded by borrowers, as suggested by Jaffee and Modigliani. Otherwise, it will adversely affect the quality of loans as suggested by Stiglitz and Weiss. This was an attempt by the authors of the credit rationing literature to explain how monetary policy works, where the loan supply curve may often become an upward sloping, backward bending supply curve. In other words, the loan supply curve beyond a certain point may become a decreasing function of the interest rate. The most important contribution of this literature is that in the process of its investigation it points out the fragility of this market.

However, it is not our view that bankers or, for that matter, lenders always try to avoid taking credit risk. In fact, taking credit risk and attempting to manage it is a regular part of the banks' operation. More importantly, the different levels of credit risk that banks take for different groups of borrowers, cause a serious difficulty for the authors of this literature to convince not only economists across the board, but also policy makers, as to why banks deny loans to some borrowers. After all, it is the latter factor which causes a variation in the access to the loan market for different groups of borrowers. In the absence of any satisfactory explanation of the above issue, more weight was given to the argument that the imperfect competitive market and the ceiling on interest rates were the principal reasons for the observed variations in the borrowers' access to the loan market. Accordingly, policy prescribed that the removal of the ceiling on the interest rate and an injection of greater competition would not only remove the variation in the access to this market but also in turn would produce a higher growth rate than that which we observe when the economy operates under government intervention. But it was not recognized that the variation in the access to the loan market, which arises from different borrowers offering different levels of expected rates of return on loans, is unlikely to be removed by liberalizing the interest rate or by increased competition in the lenders' market for clients. In fact such policies can increase the fragility of this sector. It is to this problem we turn now.

NOTES

1. The concept of cash reserves captures the notion of bankers' unwillingness to reduce the liquidity of their portfolios, and also reflects the constraints that often emerge as a result of the central bank's capital adequacy requirements. Banks' unwillingness to reduce the liquidity of their portfolios principally arises from the fact that public confidence in banks depends on the belief that they will always be able to exchange deposits for cash demands. This power to offer cash in exchange for deposits is the prerequisite of the profit which a bank seeks. Thus liquidity refers to the bankers' ability to satisfy demands for cash in exchange for deposits. To earn profits, banks must gain public confidence and to maintain this confidence they must maintain an adequate degree of liquidity in their assets. See Sayers (1960a) for further details.

2. It is not our view that a borrower's attitude towards risk cannot play any role in determining the fate of the loan capital, nor do we deny that there may exist some relationship between an individual's attitude towards risk and his/her pecuniary position. But to use pecuniary position as a proxy for, or as a possible determinant of, the direction of the attitude towards risk, may be demanding too much. It is similar to predicting whether Schrodinger's cat is dead or alive, prior to opening the box. Let me elaborate on this issue; usually it is assumed that in an investment project, if a borrower's own wealth constitutes a small fraction of the total investment, then that borrower is likely to take a greater risk, since that borrower has less to lose in the event of a project failure. In other words, the interpretation here is that the attitude towards risk is inversely related to the borrower's pecuniary position. Thus the argument here is that although an individual's attitude towards risk is not known, if we know his/her pecuniary position, then the direction of the attitude towards risk can be predicted. This is what we call the hidden variable approach to uncertainty analysis. The problem with this approach is that once we incorporate further information or rearrange the information set within the frame of the hidden variable analysis, our result will change, as we have shown in the previous chapter. For example, suppose there is a poor investor whose share of capital constitutes a very small fraction of the total investment, but whose entire livelihood depends on the return from this share. On this occasion can we hold the same inverse relationship between attitude towards risk and pecuniary position of the person concerned? Similarly, it can be shown that a wealthy investor is more likely to take a greater risk, independent of the share of his/her own capital in the investment project, if that share constitutes an insignificant fraction of his/her total wealth. The above example highlights the problem, i.e. as we change our information set our result continues to change, and this raises the question of whether the uncertainty is associated with the hidden variable or arises from the missing information. In reality of course, we know neither what governs an individual's attitude towards risk nor the impact of external variables, such as the pecuniary position, on an internal variable such as the attitude towards risk. A further complication of the problem also arises from the fact that an individual's attitude towards risk changes over time and space, independent of his/her pecuniary position. Therefore, whatever our subjective opinion may be about the individual's attitude towards risk, it cannot be predicted accurately from the individual's pecuniary position, although we cannot ignore the importance of the latter factor in the consideration of the loan equation. The problem of uncertainty is not associated with some

hidden variable as apprears to be the case in the asymmetric information literature. Whether we follow the Copenhagen (i.e. Bohr, Heisenberg, Schrodinger, etc.) or Keynes's interpretation of uncertainty, in both cases the explanation of uncertainty rests on the assumption of missing information or what we call incomplete information and it is associated with space and time. Even von Neumann, whose work has been extensively used in the asymmetric information literature, ruled out the possibility of the hidden variable interpretation as a possible explanation for uncertainty. See Heisenberg (1958), Pais (1991), Gribbin (1995/1999) and Davies (1995) for the Copenhagen interpretation of the uncertainty principle.

3. Let me explain the above point with the help of a housing mortgage. In this instance, the size of the loan is determined by the borrower's capacity to pay, which is determined by the current income derived from current employment. A loan is advanced neither on the basis of the expected return from the rent of the house, nor on the basis of the future value of the house. The house and the deposit are used as alternative assets; that is, should the borrower lose his/her current employment, or for some reason be unable to maintain the repayments, then the bank will sell the house to recoup the loan capital. In this instance, while the borrower is more likely to lose the amount of loan already paid plus the deposit, the bank is not likely to lose any of its loan capital. However, if the bank would have lent on the basis of the expected return from the house, irrespective of the borrower's income and without any deposit requirements, then for such a loan, although the house has been used as collateral, banks carry the entire risk. That is, should the borrower default, he/she has nothing to lose and the recovery of the loan capital entirely depends on the value of the house at that time, which is not known. Thus on this occasion, although the house can be used as collateral, it does not meet the attributes of the credit standard.

4. The cost side is also subject to uncertainty from the configuration of the price of inputs. For the sake of simplicity we have assumed the cost to be constant.

5. At any point in time the consumer's choice of products, other than for minimum essentials, is mostly subject to income constraints. This implies that tastes and preferences are not unchanging variables as they are influenced by an individual's own choice, subject to income constraints (or we can say it is subject to the individual's income) and influenced by his/her social background. Although consumption is largely a function of habit, habits do not remain constant over the life of a consumer. Furthermore habits are not independent of income, price and social background. Thus we can say that in the formation of habit, a consumer's income and his/her social background do play a role (Hahn, 1985). From the above it follows that changes in income in general will alter consumers' preferences, which in turn will have a different effect on the demand for different commodities (Passinetti, 1981 and 1993). Furthermore, the prediction of future demand is based on current consumers' preferences, but does not include those who are now too young to express any preferences. Thus the prediction of future demand that assumes there will be no divergence between that of current and future consumers appears to rely on too demanding (or exacting) an assumption. See Sen (1984a) on this issue, although it is discussed in a different context.

6. In fact, it was these problems that led Bhaduri (1990) to argue that the cost factor plays a decisive role in the determination of price. This is because of the fact that the entrepreneurs not only have some control over the cost but more importantly, as Bhaduri argues, they also have more hard information about the cost. This lends support to Kalecki's (1971) argument that the prices of the finished products are cost-determined.

7. See Coveney and Highfield (1991) for further on the irreversibility of time, see also Kregel (1978).

8. It is important to make a distinction between risk and uncertainty. A risky event

refers to a situation where there is sufficient information to assign probability. Uncertainty refers to a situation where there is not enough information (i.e. incomplete information). This distinction was clearly identified by Keynes (1973, pp. 113–114), when he wrote, 'By "uncertainty" knowledge, let me explain I do not mean merely to distinguish what is known for certain from what is only probable. ... The sense in which I am using the term is that in which the prospect of a European war is uncertain, ... or the position of private wealth owners in the social system in 1970. About these matters there is no scientific basis on which to form any calculable probability whatever. We simply do not know.' In other words, as Lawson (1985, p. 915) puts it, 'For example if I purchase one out of a million lottery tickets, then the hypothesis that my ticket will be "drawn" has many rivals, but given the evidence available to me (one million lottery tickets and a "fair" draw) the hypothesis that I shall win, though improbable, is not uncertain. However, if I do not know the number of lottery tickets and I have no information about this number, then the hypothesis that I shall win is uncertain.' See Basu (1994, 1996 and 2001) also on this issue.

9. See Basu (1994) for further on the above issue.

10. Meltzer (1988, pp. 145–46) notes that statisticians and economists in general have not accepted the Keynes–Knight distinction between risk and uncertainty. He writes, 'A main reason is that these terms do not have independent meaning in modern theories of statistical decision making. I believe the Keynes–Knight notion is dismissed too readily. The distinction between risk and uncertainty can be treated as a difference in the (subjective) probability distribution and the information that people use when making decisions. Uncertainty can be represented by a very diffuse prior probability distribution assigned to the returns that will be earned and the states in which they will be earned in the distant future. Risk can refer to near-term prospects where the probability distribution is much less diffuse. As Keynes said in the preceding passage, the only near-term risk is that the news will change, and he added that the change is 'unlikely to be very large'. Much less is known, according to Keynes, about long-term prospects. Since people must make decisions, they act as if they know the probabilities or the distribution of returns when, in truth, the (subjective) prior probability assigned to any particular outcome in the distant future is small and the probability distribution is diffuse. Diffuse uncertainty about long-term events would be non-diversifiable and therefore non-insurable by the owners of a firm. Hence it fits the criterion for uncertainty in the Keynes–Knight terminology.' While Meltzer's and Hicks's (1979, p. 69) distinction between risk and uncertainty, i.e. 'Increased dispersion means increased uncertainty' is questionable, the important issue is that they acknowledge the issue of uncertainty. See also Boulding (1962), Georgescu-Roegen (1971), and Machina (1987); in particular the former two authors' work addresses the 'uncertainty principle' that was proven by Heisenberg (1930, 1958).

11. As Samuelson wrote (1966, p. 1757), 'it is clear that no prior empirical truths can exist in any field. If a thing has a prior irrefutable truth, it must be empty of empirical content. It must be regarded as a meaningless proposition in the technical sense of modern philosophy.' Furthermore Keynes wrote (1936, pp. 162–63), 'that human decisions affecting the future, whether personal or political or economic, cannot depend on strict mathematical expectation, since the basis for making such calculations does not exist; and that it is our innate urge to activity which makes the wheels go round, our rational selves choosing between the alternatives as best we are able, calculating where we can, but often falling back for our motive on whim or sentiment or chance.'

12. One may argue that lenders in this situation may use information from future markets or business expectation surveys. The problem with the former is that future buying

or selling both rely on the expectation that the future price will be higher or lower than the contractual price. Thus the problem remains that if the actual price becomes lower than the contractual price, then in the case of forward buying, the buyer will lose. A similar problem also remains in the case of forward selling. With business expectation surveys, a similar problem arises again, as all of these expectations are formed on the basis of the current and immediate past economic performance of the countries concerned. In the absence of any future information, these expectations are subject to the same error that we have explained above.

13. See De Meza and Webb (1987) on this issue, although their results follow in circumstances where there is asymmetric information, while our argument is centred on the notion of pure uncertainty.

14. See also Azzi and Cox (1976) on this issue.

15. For example, the unemployed person, who has no income other than social security for his/her survival may desire a credit card, but is unlikely to receive one. Jappelli (1990) points out that in the United States the lowest income group has the lowest access to the loan market, largely because of their lower asset backing.

16. For example, in Australia, banks normally lend 80 to 95 percent of the current market value of the house, depending on which lending institution one is dealing with, and that institution's confidence about the state of the economy. The convention behind this policy is that no one knows what the value of such property will be in 10 or 20 years time; however past observations reveal that the property value is unlikely to fall by 5 to 20 percent in the near future, say within the next 2 to 3 years. Thus if the price falls by that margin banks can still recoup the principal by selling the property. However, if the borrower defaults on the loan, say 10 years from today (assuming such a borrower has not accumulated any appreciable further debt), then it is unlikely that the borrower will owe any appreciable amount of principal which cannot be paid from the proceeds of the property. Contrary to the above, recent experience in the case of Australian agriculture shows that at times the current market value of a property can fall to such a level that the sale of the property is unlikely to cover to any appreciable extent, the principal these borrowers owe to banks.

17. See for example, Chase (1961), whose explanation of rationing, resting on the argument that the return on investment is not monotonically related to the size of the investment while the contractual payment is a function of interest rate and the size of the loan, is clearly describing the factor giving rise to default risk, but refers to it as credit risk. See also Ryder (1962) and various textbooks in this context, for example Sinkey (1989).

18. Expressed as a percentage of the ratio of credit risk to loan capital (i.e. principal plus interest rate).

19. The above analysis follows from the Smithian notion of competition which Coase (1977, p. 318) described, 'as rivalry, as a process, rather than as a condition defined by a high elasticity of demand, as would be true for most modern economists'.

20. Gertler and Gilchrist (1994) reveal that a firm's reliance on bank finance as an external source of funds falls as the firm's asset size grows larger. For example, for a firm with an asset size of less than $50 million, 68 percent of the total debt is comprised of bank loans, as opposed to a firm with an asset size of $50–250 million, where only 55 percent of the external funds come from a bank. For firms with an asset size of $250–1000 and over $1000 million respectively, it is 40 and 17 percent respectively. On the other hand, Scherer (1980) found the debt cost varied with the size of the asset, and corporations with assets of $200 million borrowed funds at an average interest rate of 0.74 percentage points lower than the firms with assets of $5 million. Billion-dollar corporations enjoyed a 0.34 point incremental advantage over their $200 million asset counterparts. This latter factor principally arises from the lower transaction cost. See Basu (1989) for further discussion on this issue.

4. Financial liberalization[1]

4.1 INTRODUCTION

McKinnon (1973) and Shaw (1973) provide a theoretical explanation as to why a mandatory ceiling on interest rates, and numerous lending restrictions that have been imposed on the banks, may have caused variations in access to the loan market for different groups of borrowers. In Chapter 2 we argued that this explanation is not adequate. However their argument is not confined to the issue of credit rationing, but extends to an explanation of how these regulations in turn may adversely affect the growth rate. They argue that a ceiling on interest rates which is below that of the market clearing rate, depresses savings, thereby reducing the availability of funds for investment growth, and encourages investors to undertake low yield investments, resulting in a low growth rate. Thus the essential argument is that financial repression causes low growth rate. Accordingly, they recommend financial liberalization, often referred to as deregulation, which involves lifting the ceiling on interest rates, the removal of various lending restrictions that were previously imposed on banks and the removal of barriers to entry, and suggest that this course of action will produce a higher growth rate. While McKinnon and Shaw mainly focus on exogenous factors (e.g. the impact of government intervention on financial markets), the recent literature following this line of thought focuses on the endogenous process, that is, in the absence of intervention how the endogenous process will produce a higher growth rate. This in turn gives further credence to McKinnon's and Shaw's thesis. We will now examine the general hypothesis that liberalization will promote growth, in light of the two concepts that have been developed in our previous chapter, namely the credit standard and credit risk.

The basic tenet of liberalization is centred on the postulation that there is an explicit link between financial development and growth rate. Goldsmith (1969) observes that there was an upward drift in the ratio of financial institutions' assets to GNP for 35 countries, including both developed and less developed countries, between 1860 and 1963. Interestingly, he also observes that in the early stage of development, banks' finance played a crucial role; however in the later stage of development, the importance of banks to some extent declined, as a result of the growth of either the NBFI or the stock market. However, Goldsmith is very cautious in deriving any particular conclusion from this observation as to whether financial factors were primarily responsible for the acceleration of economic development or whether the financial development reflected economic growth. In Goldsmith, the process of growth has a feedback impact on the financial sector, as he observes that the process of growth itself creates incentives for further financial development and this gives the impression that financial intermediation may be an endogenous process.

Following the development of the endogenous growth model (Romer, 1986 and 1990), recent literature on finance and development has incorporated the role of financial factors within the framework of this model, where financial intermediation is also considered as an endogenous process. The main feature of endogenous growth models is that technological change is assumed to be an endogenous process; as a result capital stock does not necessarily suffer from a diminishing return, and consequently growth becomes a positive function of investment (Fry, 1997). The proponents of models that take financial intermediation and growth as endogenous, argue that there exists a positive two-way causal relationship between economic growth and financial development. The essential argument in this literature is that the process of growth encourages higher participation in the financial markets, which in turn facilitates the creation and the expansion of financial institutions. It is also argued that financial institutions, by collecting and analysing information from potential borrowers, enable the allocation of funds for investment projects to be more efficient and thus promote investment and growth (Greenwood and Jovanovic, 1990).

Banks and other NBFI play a crucial role in the process of development. These financial intermediaries open up the opportunity for individuals to hold their savings in the form of deposits, thereby reducing the need to hold them in the form of illiquid unproductive tangible assets, thus increasing liquidity in the economy. Banks then can use these deposits to invest in currency and capital. While an individual's need for liquidity remains unpredictable, banks, by the law of large numbers, face a predictable demand for deposit withdrawals, and this in turn allows banks to invest funds more efficiently. In other words, by applying the law of large numbers, banks can avoid the unnecessary premature liquidation of capital that otherwise would emerge with the absence of banks, where individual investors may be forced to liquidate their assets prematurely when liquidity needs arise. Thus banks avoid resource misallocation, provide liquidity to savers and at the same time offer long term funds to investors. Hence the essence of the argument is that inducing savers to switch from unproductive assets to productive assets must stimulate productive investment.[2] Accordingly King and Levine (1993a, p. 517) argue that, 'Financial repression . . . reduces the services provided by the financial system to savers, entrepreneurs, and producers; it thereby impedes innovative activity and slows economic growth.'[3]

The most important contribution of this literature is that it points out the active and positive role that financial factors play in the process of economic development.[4] In order to highlight this aspect of finance, the focus is on the interest rate as a primary channel for intermediation between savings, investment and growth. But the authors of this literature overlook the crucial role that the credit standard and credit risk play in the process of intermediation between savings and investment,[5] a consideration of which may suggest that the result that they derived may not be achieved via liberalization.

It is argued in this literature that in the liberalized system, competition between lending institutions for depositors will cause a rise in the interest rate on deposits, which in turn will raise the deposits. In other words, higher interest rates will induce households to increase their level of savings. This in turn will increase the availability of credit and thereby will cause a rise in investment growth. Furthermore, it is argued that although investment responds to the interest rate negatively, the growth rate responds to the interest rate positively. It is argued that as the higher interest rate discourages low return investment, investors will be induced to undertake high return investments, thereby bringing efficiency to investment, which in turn will improve the growth rate to a greater extent than that which is possible under financial repression. Thus the key link here is the interest rate. Now let us briefly examine whether the interest rate alone can play such a crucial link between savings, investment and growth rate.

4.2   ARE SAVINGS A FUNCTION OF INTEREST RATE?

To begin with, it is assumed that savings are a function of interest rate. Extensive empirical investigations so far have been unable to produce any conclusive evidence to support this assumption. For example, Fry (1978 and 1980) in a sample of fourteen Asian developing countries and Turkey, found the existence of a positive relationship between the interest rate and savings ratios. Giovannini (1983) reproduced Fry's equation using the same set of seven Asian countries, but applied it to a different sample period, and found that Fry's result could not be obtained in a different sample period. This raises some serious doubts about the evidence that was produced by Fry. Gupta (1987) did further tests using 22 Asian and Latin American countries, and while he found support for income growth as a determinant of savings, he could not find much support for the above hypothesis. Interestingly, Gupta observed that the results revealed a significant regional variation. There could be two possible explanations for this; one being that if two regions have a different growth in income then it is reasonable to assume they should produce a different savings rate, other things being equal. The second possible explanation is that this variation may have emerged due to the fact that, as Khatkhate (1988) and Cho (1989) observed, a higher interest rate mainly helps in the mobilization of savings. In other words, a higher interest rate changes the composition of savings portfolios, i.e. the savings that were previously held in the form of inventory will now be transformed into financial assets. In this situation, the impact of the interest rate on the mobilization of savings will largely be determined by the value of the savings that were held in the form of inventory. Thus if two nations have two different levels of inventories, changes in the interest rate are likely to reveal different levels of savings. It is the second possible explanation which may also provide a clue as to why Giovannini's different sample period produced a result that is in sharp contrast to the result obtained by Fry. Interestingly, Demetriades and Luintel (1996) found that the extension of branch facilities played a positive role in the mobilization of savings in the case of India.[6] This inconclusive nature of the findings may have led Modigliani (1986, p. 304) to conclude that, 'despite a hot debate, no convincing general evidence either way has been produced, which leads me to the provisional view that s [the savings ratio] is largely independent of the interest rate.' Common sense suggests that a person who has an insufficient income and struggles to survive on a basic diet will never be able to save, irrespective of the level of interest rate; for example, the poor people in India. Marshall made this point abundantly clear as he wrote (1920, p. 190), 'The power to save depends on an excess of income over necessary expenditure and this is greatest among the wealthy.' On the other hand, if we assume that we save for our future consumption, then a higher interest rate instead of inducing us to raise our level of savings should in fact reduce our urge to save.[7]

The above argument simply suggests that savings are residual and arise from the difference between income and consumption. Allocation of savings is largely governed by the level of interest rate, liquidity preference and our taste and preference for risk and uncertainty. This argument therefore may explain why empirical investigations are unable to establish a direct link between interest rate and savings. If interest rate plays any role in inducing higher levels of savings, its role is a minor one.

4.3   THE RELATIONSHIP BETWEEN AVAILABILITY OF CREDIT AND INVESTMENT GROWTH

Regarding the relationship between the availability of credit and investment growth, it is also assumed that the interest rate plays a key linking role. In other words, the interest rate intermediates between savers and investors, or more precisely, lenders and borrowers relate via the interest rate. The crucial assumption behind this argument is that there is certainty about the loan repayment. Given this assumption, we do not need to make a distinction between the availability of credit and access to credit, as a rise in the former will automatically improve the latter.

But the problem here is a critical one, and we will be using the analysis developed in the previous chapter to investigate this issue. We pointed out in the first section of Chapter 3 that the loan market operates in the presence of uncertainty. This uncertainty principally arises from the fact that there remains a time gap between the advancement and repayment of loans. In this situation loan advancement will be based on the assumption that the borrower's (i.e. investor's) expected proceeds from the project will be sufficient to repay the principal plus interest. But owing to the presence of uncertainty, neither the investor nor the lender can calculate the expected value of a project's outcome with absolute accuracy. In other words, there remains a possibility that the expected value may deviate from its actual value.[8] This in turn introduces the possibility that the borrower may not be able to honour his/her promises.

This introduces the need for the separation of the concept of availability of credit from that of access to credit. In other words, as uncertainty enters into the equation in relation to the loan repayment, it is implied that promises to pay the interest rate alone cannot clear the loan market. Lenders have to take measures to ensure that should the borrower's project fail, they do not lose their loan capital. Therefore, the credit standard enters into the loan equation as a means of protecting the loan capital in the event of failure. In this situation, loan approval will depend on whether the borrower can meet the bank's credit standard, and this is independent of the merits of the project.

Now given this analysis, let us assume the interest rate increases as a result of liberalization.[9] This will increase the deposits, either as a result of a change in the composition of savings portfolios where savers prefer to hold financial assets as opposed to unproductive assets, or as a result of a rise in the access to the foreign savings market, resulting in a rise in the availability of credit. But the rise in the deposit rate will also cause a rise in the loan rate, and with a given size of loan, this in turn will also increase the contractual repayment rate. This means the credit standard that has been set in accordance with the size of the loan and the previous interest rate, is no longer capable of protecting the bank's entire loan capital when the interest rate increases. In this situation, the portion of the loan which is not secured by the credit standard is that portion of the contractual repayment rate which has increased as a result of a rise in the loan rate. The portion, which is not secured by the credit standard, will not be recouped from the proceeds of the collateral. In other words, all things being equal, a rise in the interest rate will cause a rise in the credit risk. We are assuming banks' main aim is to protect the entire loan capital by the credit standard, so that no shortfall will arise in meeting the depositors' demand should there be a failure in borrowers' projects. In other words banks would like to take a zero credit risk. Thus banks will raise the credit standard to the level where the credit risk becomes zero.[10] If some borrowers cannot meet this higher credit standard, then they will receive loans of a lesser size than demanded or will be denied loans altogether, which is consistent with the findings of the credit rationing literature. This means a rise in the availability of credit does not necessarily imply a rise in the borrowers' access to the loan market. In fact as just shown above, a rise in the availability of credit can be accompanied by a reduction in access to the loan market for some borrowers who may have qualified for the loan previously.[11]

However, we pointed out in Chapter 3 that the level of credit risk that banks wish to take is not entirely determined by their taste and preference for risk and uncertainty, but rather is determined in conjunction with the competitive atmosphere in which they operate. We argue that the level of competition that banks face varies from one borrowing group to another and arises from the fact that different borrowing groups offer different levels of expected profitability on loans. Large borrowers in general offer higher expected rates of return per unit of loan than their smaller counterparts. As we pointed out in our previous chapter, this is due to combinations of three of the following factors: (a) large borrowers demand loans of a larger size, which in turn reduces the transaction cost on these loans; (b) due to economies of scale of operation and greater control over the prices of their product, they are less vulnerable to the adverse shock that may follow from, for example, fluctuations in the aggregate demand, compared with their smaller counterparts; and (c) in addition to this, as they have assets of greater value and this suggests that even if the project's (for which they seek loans) return falls below the expected level, they have more than sufficient alternative means to maintain their contractual payment. The combined impact of the lower administrative cost and a lower possibility of default, offers a much higher level of expected rate of return on larger loans than any smaller loans.

The demand for borrowers who offer a higher expected rate of return, with a given level of interest rate, will be high in the lenders' market compared with those who offer a lower expected rate of return on loans. This higher demand in turn provides a choice to those borrowers who offer a higher expected rate of return on loans. That is, they can either borrow from banks or from other lending institutions, and can also raise funds directly from the stock market. Thus when competing for these clients as borrowers in the lenders' market, banks have no option other than to make concessions in order to attract them, including relaxation of the credit standard requirements, interest rate concessions and better terms and conditions for the loan repayment. However, as the borrowers' ability to offer higher expected rates of return falls, given the level of interest rate, with a decreasing size of operation and with lower asset backing, the demand for such borrowers falls in the lenders' market. This means these borrowers will have less choice in raising external funds from alternative sources. In a majority of cases, most borrowers have the option either to raise external capital by borrowing from banks or by borrowing from friends and relatives. Those borrowers who do not have access to the banks' loan market seek loans either from private moneylenders or from friends and relatives. Thus as their choice of alternative means to raise external funds shrinks, there is an increase in the banks' monopoly power over such borrowers and this power shrinks as borrowers' ability to offer higher expected rates of return increases. Accordingly, where banks have a monopoly power they will set the credit standard at a level where the credit risk will be zero, and as the monopoly power erodes so too does their ability to insist on credit standards that can fully secure their loan capital. This therefore suggests that not all borrowers will have equal access to the loan market.

Now given this analysis, suppose the interest rate and the competition between the lending institutions increase as a result of liberalization. However according to our above analysis, this competition is likely to be concentrated in the large borrowers' loan market, thereby leaving little or no spillover effect of this greater competition to be felt in the small borrowers' loan market. This means banks' monopoly or near monopoly power is unlikely to be affected as a result of the greater competition, when dealing with smaller and medium sized borrowers who demand smaller loans. Therefore, banks will raise the credit standard for smaller borrowers, simply because the interest rate and credit standard are interdependent variables. If they fail to meet the banks' new credit standard, then either their access will be denied or they will receive less than that demanded. But banks' ability to raise the credit standard for those who seek large loans will be further restricted by the higher level of competition that follows from liberalization of the lenders' market. This therefore suggests that if liberalization increases the interest rate then it is more likely that the smaller and medium sized borrowers' access to the banks' loan market will be reduced. For example, Jaramillo *et al.* (1996) investigated whether there was any improvement in small firms' access to the loan market during the post-liberalization period as opposed to the pre-liberalized period, for Ecuadorian firms. Their investigation was based on a rich panel data set containing balance sheets and profit and loss statements for 420 manufacturing companies during the period 1983–88. Of these firms, 22 percent were considered to be large, with assets over US$600,000 (at 1975 prices) and 47 percent of the sample was represented by young firms, i.e. those who were established after 1970. The dividing line between the pre- and post-liberalization period was taken as 1986 on the basis of the fact that the interest rate was fully deregulated in 1986 and the real rate reached positive levels. They found that while there was no change in access to the loan market either in the pre- or post-liberalization periods for the large firms, the small and young firms had difficulties in gaining access to it in both periods and these difficulties further increased during the post-liberalization period.[12] This was mainly because these borrowers are often unable to meet banks' higher credit standards. On the other hand, as liberalization increases the competition among the lending institutions for large borrowers as clients, banks have to relax their credit standard requirements even further than they would have done in the absence of liberalization. This therefore suggests that liberalization not only further aggravates the unequal access to the loan market beyond that which already exists,[13] but also makes the banking system fragile as the loan portfolios carry a higher level of credit risk than they would have done in the absence of liberalization.

The above analysis suggests that the second link that was proposed by the proponents of the school of liberalization is not tenable. But more importantly, this policy has potential, firstly, to further aggravate the unequal access to the loan market that already exists and, secondly, to increase this sector's vulnerability.

4.4   IS IT POSSIBLE TO SWITCH BETWEEN PROJECTS AT ZERO COST?

Now let us examine their third link, which is that higher interest rates will encourage investors to undertake high return investments, while discouraging low return investments, which in turn will bring efficiency in the growth rate. This proposition is based on simple logic, i.e. as the higher interest rate reduces the net return for projects that succeed, it therefore will induce investors to switch from low return to high return projects. Thus the question here is whether the higher interest rate will induce investors to undertake high return investments, since lower return investments reduce the net return in the presence of higher interest rates. In other words, in order to maintain at least the same level of net return, will investors switch from low return to high return investments? The crucial assumption therefore is that the selection of a project varies with the level of interest rate. Central to this assumption is the claim that a higher interest rate will improve the growth rate.

In the third section of Chapter 2 we investigated this possibility, that is, whether changes in the interest rate can induce investors to switch from low return to high return investments. Our analysis suggests that such a switch involves additional costs that are associated with the selection of, and switching between, projects. The former arise because of the costs involved in the gathering information in relation to the expected return of all the alternative available projects necessary for the selection of a project. The latter costs arise as the switch involves disposing of the old project in favour of the new one. The cost of dispossession of the old project principally arises because investment expenditure is largely irreversible. That is, these are mostly sunk costs and therefore cannot be recovered. Thus if an investor decides to switch from his/her old project to a new project then he/she has to take into consideration the net loss that will be incurred from the dispossession of the old project. This cost must be included in addition to the cost that will be incurred in acquiring a new project, and we refer to these costs as switching costs. We argue that once we include the selection and the switching costs, the net return of a new project may not be able to compensate sufficiently for the net loss that will be incurred as a result of a switch. This problem is further complicated by the fact that if all firms decide to switch from a low return to a high return project, then investors have to incur a further capital loss in the old project, as they have to sell it below the book value in order to induce other investors to buy. Furthermore, as a large number of investors will be switching from low return to high return projects, then these projects' net return may not remain high due to the crowding out effect. Thus we argue that the higher interest rate may not be able to induce investors to switch from low return projects to high return projects. This argument is equally applicable to the present case also. This therefore suggests that the investors who are directly engaged in producing either goods or services, may not be able to switch from one project to another in the event of changes in the interest rate.[14] It therefore follows that the higher interest rate, or liberalization for that matter, is unlikely to deliver a higher growth rate.

In fact, in the case of Latin America, De Gregorio and Guidotti (1995) found the existence of a very strong negative correlation between financial intermediation and growth during the 1970s and 1980s, a period when their financial market was liberalized. Real GDP in Argentina declined by 11 percent between 1980 and 1982, in Chile by 15 percent between 1981 and 1983 and in Uruguay by 14 percent between 1980 and 1983 (Diaz-Alejandro, 1985). Similarly, in Mexico, the GDP growth rate declined by 20 percent between 1994 and 1995. In Thailand, Malaysia, South Korea and Indonesia, the GDP growth rate declined by 10 percent between 1996 and 1998 (Miskin, 1999). A study by Arestis and Glickman (2002) also found that in Thailand, South Korea, Indonesia, Malaysia and the Philippines the GDP growth rate declined by almost 11 percent between 1995 and 1998.

The problem with financial liberalization is that it opens up the opportunity for investors who carry substantial financial assets in their portfolio to take advantage of higher interest rates and a greater flow of credit.[15] The financial assets do not have a direct link, as their link with physical capital is an indirect one via the purchase of shares, and therefore the sale of these will not incur a sunk cost. But it may often involve a capital loss if they wish to switch from a low yield to a high yield investment when the interest rate increases (for reasons already explained above). In other words, in the absence of sunk costs, the total capital loss that will be incurred is much lower than that incurred by an investor who is involved in a productive activity and who wishes to sell his/her investment in order to switch to a new venture. This therefore suggests that investors who carry portfolio investments will have the opportunity to switch from low yield securities to high yield securities when the interest rate increases. Of course this will depend on whether the high yield securities can compensate for the capital loss that will be incurred as a result of the switch.

As large investors in general also carry a large investment portfolio they will be in a position to take advantage of this high interest rate. These are the investors who are also likely to carry high levels of credit risk. The issue here is not whether they will switch from low yield to high yield securities, but whether this greater flow of credit to the stock market will be accompanied by an equivalent rise in the supply of new shares. As the latter does not depend on the former, but on the growth of the corporate sector, which in general depends on overall economic growth, it is unlikely that this greater flow of credit will be accompanied by a rise in the supply of new shares. In this situation it is more likely that the greater flow of credit will cause a rise in the price of shares. This in turn introduces the possibility of making a profit from the expected increase in price. As the profit from the purchase and subsequent sale of shares rises, loan capital will be further attracted to the stock market, thereby increasing the stock market activity. This introduces the possibility of attracting a substantial portion of the banks' loan capital to move away from the productive areas of the economy in favour of financial assets.[16] This obviously raises a concern about the efficiency gain via liberalization.[17] Furthermore, in the process, as the link between the share market and the real sector gets weaker, share prices will tend to deviate substantially from the fundamentals on which the initial share price was set. In other words, the yield on shares will not be able to justify their rise in price. More importantly, in this process the return on loans will no longer be linked with the yield from shares; rather it will be inter-locked with the return from the expected change in the price of shares.

This is where a serious problem arises, and that is, if the actual price falls short of the expected price, then these borrowers may have difficulty in meeting their commitment to banks. In this situation banks will not be able to recoup the entire portion of the loan capital from the proceeds of the collateral. This problem arises because the banks cannot maintain their credit standard requirements for these borrowers. In other words, banks have advanced loans which exceed the aggregate value of the borrowers' assets. Thus the core of the problem lies with the fact that banks have had to take a higher level of credit risk on large loans as a result of liberalization.[18]

4.5 CONCLUSION

A careful examination of the issues involved suggests that the link that the school of liberalization has claimed to have established via the interest rate under the free market mechanism, cannot be established via the interest rate alone. This therefore may suggest that the policy of financial liberalization is unlikely to produce a higher growth rate. Instead, as the process of liberalization raises the interest rate, this will cause a rise in the banks' credit standard requirements for smaller and medium sized firms. This in turn will aggravate unequal access to the loan market even further. In addition, the overall credit standard requirements will fall largely as a result of a relaxation in these requirements for large borrowers. Thus if these borrowers default on loans then a substantial portion of the principal will not be recouped from the sale of collateral. It is this possibility which introduces the seeds of financial crisis.

NOTES

1. For an abridged version of this chapter and Chapter 5 see Basu (2002, forthcoming).
2. See also Bencivenga and Smith (1991), Levine (1992), King and Levine (1993a, b), Saint-Paul (1992) and Roubini and Sala-i-Martin (1992). A number of authors (Roubini and Sala-i-Martin, 1992; King and Levine, 1993a, b; Fry, 1997), including the World Bank (1989), have empirically investigated the above relationships and found a positive result. However, as Arestis and Demetriades (1996) point out, King and Levine's work was probably the most well known, but their method was based on cross-section data in relation to causality effect. Subsequently Arestis and Demetriades (1996) used the time series analysis for 12 countries (France, Germany,

UK, Japan, USA, Korea, India, Greece, Spain, Turkey, Mexico and Chile) and found that the causal link between finance and growth depends upon the nature and operation of the financial institutions and policies pursued by each country. (See Arestis and Demetriades, 1997 for further details).

3. Similarly, Fry (1997, p. 758), wrote that, 'discriminatory taxation of commercial banks, investment banks, mutual funds, and stock markets through high reserve requirements, interest and credit ceilings, directed credit programmes . . . reduces the growth rate by impeding financial development.' See also Roubini and Sala-i-Martin (1992) who argue that financial distortion has a negative effect. Contrary to this claim, Arestis and Demetriades (1997) found that financial repression had a positive impact upon the growth rate in the case of South Korea. Even the World Bank's (1993) report concedes that mild repression may have a positive impact on the High Performing Asian economies. One cannot draw the same conclusion from the Indian experience (Demetriades and Luintel, 1996). Rajan and Zingales (1998), on the other hand, argue that whether the development of the financial market is determined by historical accident or as a result of government regulation does not really matter, since in either case a well-developed financial market will have a beneficial impact on the industries that are dependent on external capital.

4. In economics, the role of finance in general is a passive one, the state of the art of the literature was that, 'by and large, it seems to be the case that where enterprise leads finance follows' (Robinson, 1979, p. 20). The role of finance in the context of economic development is also a much neglected area in the literature on economic development (Arndt, 1987). Lucas (1988) considered the relation between financial and economic development to be 'over stressed'. Chandavarkar (1992) provides an impressive list of authors who are pioneers in economic development, including three Nobel Laureates (e.g. Bauer, Colin Clark, Hirschman, Lewis, Myrdal, Prebisch, Rosenstein-Rodan, Rostow, Singer and Tinbergen) who also did not even mention finance as a factor in economic development. Furthermore, Chandavarkar points out that the recent surveys of economic development by Stern (1989) also ignore the role of the financial sector in the context of development.

5. Similarly, there are some authors (e.g. Bencivenga *et al.*, 1996; Levine and Zervos, 1996) who argue that there is an explicit link between the development of stock markets and long-run growth. Their argument is centred on the notion that many high return projects require long-term capital. However, investors are often reluctant to commit their savings to long-term projects. Stock markets provide the opportunity for firms to undertake long-term projects by offering liquidity to savers. That is, they issue equities to raise funds for long-term high return projects, and these equities are held by savers, who then can off load them cheaply when liquidity needs arise. Hence in the process it should promote growth. Apart from the fact that new equity issues account for a very small fraction of corporate investment (Mayer, 1988), they overlook an important issue, i.e. only firms with a well-established reputation and with a large asset backing are able to raise funds via issuing shares. This means only large corporations, big banks and other large NBFI will be able to raise funds from the stock market. An important point to note here is that offering a return or a yield on shares is not a sufficient criterion to raise funds; issuing firms must have a large asset backing. This is independent of whether it is an innovative firm or is offering a high or low return on shares. To put it mildly, entrepreneurial ability is not a sufficient criterion to obtain capital for starting a business venture. See Kalecki (1971) on this issue. In other words, the majority of businesses, comprising small and medium sized firms, including farmers, will be excluded from this market. Therefore development of the stock market would not contribute to the growth of these sectors, and thus would not improve economic welfare. Furthermore, as a sizeable part of the economy would be excluded from the stock market, it remains a difficult proposition

to prove whether or not development of the stock market would promote growth. This is irrespective of whether or not one finds a correlation between the stock market and long-run growth, since a correlation does not tell us anything about the causality of such a link, and it could be the growth which promotes the stock market. In either case the benefit from the growth of the stock market is a highly controversial issue, as other authors (e.g. Devereux and Smith, 1994 and Obstfeld, 1994) found that the internationally integrated stock market can depress saving rates, slow down the growth rate and reduce economic welfare. See also Singh (1997) for further on this issue, who suggests that on efficiency grounds evolution of the stock market should be curbed.

6. See also Dornbusch and Reynoso (1989), who found that financial savings are not related to a positive interest rate. See Arestis and Demetriades (1997) for further on this issue. For earlier work on this issue see Chandavarkar (1971), Mikesell and Zinser (1972) and Dougherty (1980). As far as financial liberalization is concerned, Diaz-Alejandro (1985) noted that domestic savings in South America did not increase as a result of liberalization. In fact, the Chilian Gross National Savings fell from 16.3 percent of GDP during the 1960s to 12.4 percent during 1975–81. Even Fry (1995, p. 158) who in his earlier work found a positive effect of interest rates in Asia, following liberalization, found this effect disappeared, as he wrote, 'even in Asia the effects appear to have diminished over the past two decades, possibly because of financial liberalization.' This might have led him to concede that the impact of interest rates on the savings ratio may not be significant.

7. See Marshall (1920) and Keynes (1936) on this issue.

8. It is important to note that while Greenwood and Jovanovic (1990), King and Levine (1993b) and Fry (1997) argue that financial intermediaries play a key role in evaluating prospective entrepreneurs and finance the most promising one, in their model these institutions' investment strategies are determined by the knowledge they have in relation to the 'current-period aggregate shock' (Fry, 1997, p. 757). But they do not recognize that there remains a possibility that the future-period shock may deviate from the current-period shock. This possibility can only be eliminated provided we assume time is reversible. But time only moves forwards; furthermore the law of entropy suggests that it may not be sufficient for the assumption of reversible time to rely on current-period aggregate shock. See Georgescu-Roegen (1971). However as they overlooked this issue, the form of the contract that institutions devised became unimportant. King and Levine (1993a, p. 516) explicitly point out that their 'model does not focus on the precise forms of contracts and institutions that provide these services.'

9. As liberalization is not only accompanied by lifting the ceiling on interest rates, but also by greater competition among the lending institutions for depositors, it is reasonable to assume that interest rates will rise following liberalization. In fact, in Australia throughout the 1980s and early 1990s, interest rates remained high following liberalization. A similar situation has also been observed in the Latin American countries.

10. For existing loans, instead of increasing the contractual repayment rate, banks may increase the repayment period, as they often do when recognizing that borrowers may have difficulty in meeting the rising repayment rate.

11. The above argument therefore may suggest why a high interest rate may have a negative supply-side effect on working capital (Taylor, 1983 and van Wijnbergen, 1983). For example, Diaz-Alejandro (1985, p. 15) pointed out that, 'In Chile gross fixed investment during the 1960s averaged 20.2 percent of GDP; during 1974–82 it reached only 15.5 percent of GDP', and this is not because of a contraction in the growth of credit. In fact, liberalization is always accompanied by a surge in the expansion of credit, for example, the domestic credit in Chile expanded by 41

percent between December 1981 and June 1982 (Diaz-Alejandro, 1985). A study by Greene and Villanueva (1991), whose samples cover 23 developing nations from 1975–87 also found a high interest rate had a significant negative effect on private investment.

12.   One of the key elements of the policy of financial liberalization is that under the free market mechanism all borrowers' access to the loan market will be improved irrespective of their age and their size of operation. Thus government assistance will not be required. Contrary to this claim, throughout the 1980s in the United States about 25 percent of all loans were either originated by government agencies or carried government guarantees. The government organized these loans in order to assist students, small businesses, housing, exports, and for a host of other worthy causes. (Stiglitz, 1993). See Jappelli (1990) who also found that the smaller and marginal borrowers' access to the loan market in the United States has not improved. Similarly, Basu (1989) observed that in Australia, despite deregulation, a variety of government programmes continued in order to ensure that smaller borrowers' access to the loan market was not adversely affected as a result of deregulation. In India, which also embraced the policy of financial liberalization from 1991, there was a growing concern not to abolish government assisted loan programmes for small businesses, because of the fear that liberalization would reduce these borrowers' access to the loan market (Sen and Vaidya, 1997). The above evidence therefore suggests that the government had to intervene in the loan market in order to ensure that the small businesses were not disadvantaged as a result of liberalization, as occurred in the US, and when these assistance schemes were removed we observe that the smaller firms' access to the loan market was further reduced, as in the case of Ecuador.

13.   For example, Diaz-Alejandro (1985, p. 9) notes that in Chile, 'The process of financial liberalization had also led to a widely noted . . . concentration of potential economic power in the hands of a few conglomerates or economic groups, which combined financial and non-financial corporations.' Similarly, Basu (1994, p. 282) in the case of Australia also notes that, 'the distribution of loans in general favoured the large borrowers rather than the smaller and medium sized borrowers'.

14.   For further discussion on this issue, see Basu (1992 and 1996b), although discussed in a different context.

15.   As Singh (1993 and 1995) observed, the 1980s financial liberalization simply led to portfolio substitution from bank deposits to tradable securities.

16.   See also Morisset (1993) who suggested that the positive effect of a rise in domestic credit as suggested by McKinnon and Shaw could equally be offset by a portfolio shift from capital goods in favour of monetary assets. This possibility principally arises from the fact that banks have an incentive to offer loans for acquisition of financial assets as opposed to fixed investments since the former increases liquidity.

17.   The issue of efficiency gain via growth in the stock market is principally based on the postulation of the switching possibility from low yield securities to high yield securities. That is, a higher interest rate may encourage investors to abandon their low yield securities in favour of high yield securities. It is this possibility which brings discipline to firms who offer a lower yield on their securities, and thereby may bring a higher form of efficiency to these firms. See King and Levine (1993a, b) and Levine and Zervos (1996, 1998) on this argument. But in reality this involves investors switching from low yield productive investment facilities to high yield productive facilities. However, due to the irreversibility of investment expenditure, considerable doubt remains as to whether investors will be able to make adjustments that are to the satisfaction of the shareholders, quickly enough. This limits the efficiency gain through stock market activity; perhaps we are asking too much from the stock market. Conveniently, we often ignore the other observed fact, which is that

much of the stock market activity is not particularly followed by the fundamentals of securities but rather by expected changes in the price of stocks. This concerned Singh (1997), following Nagaraj (1996) in the case of India, who noted that despite the stock market boom in the 1980s, and the substantial resources raised by Indian corporations, their investment in fixed assets actually declined.

18. This may have caused the banking crisis to emerge following liberalization of the financial market. Between 1976 and 1996, there were 59 banking crashes in developing countries and the total cost of these crashes was $250 billion, which is over 9 percent of the GDP (Capiro and Honohan, 1999). This is without taking account of the Asian crisis. The banking crisis was not confined to developing countries, but has also been observed in developed nations. For example, between 1976 and 1993, there were 104 incidences of large bank failures, in 24 developed nations (Goodhart, 1995). In the USA, altogether 1150 commercial and savings banks failed between 1983 and 1990 (Benston and Kaufman, 1997). For an analysis of bank failures see Basu (1998), Calomiris and Mason (1997) and Kaminsky and Reinhart (1999). See also Hellman *et al.* (2000), where these authors argue that it is important to introduce an interest rate ceiling on deposit rates to reduce excessive competition among lending institutions for depositors, which in turn may minimize the possibility of financial crisis.

5. Intervention I: The South Korean experience

5.1 INTRODUCTION

In the last chapter we provided an explanation for why financial liberalization, despite its claims, is unlikely to deliver a higher growth rate or efficiency in the financial sector. This means some form of intervention is required in the operation of the financial sector, especially in developing countries, in order to promote growth. In recent years, there has been a growing body of literature which rightly points out why intervention is necessary and its beneficial effect in promoting growth.[1] However, experience suggests that in the past, intervention adversely affected the performance of the financial sector. This means there is a problem, particularly in the form of the intervention that has been introduced, but the existing literature seems to be somewhat limited in its ability to assist in the investigation of the negative aspects of intervention. Thus the purpose of this, and the next, chapter is to investigate what went wrong with the intervention and why. In this chapter we will investigate this issue with reference to South Korea.

South Korea is one of the most successful nations, in terms of its economic performance, where government intervention played a positive role in the process of development. Yet it also followed the path of liberalization. In fact, financial liberalization followed by financial crisis can be traced back to weaknesses that seemed to creep in during the period of intervention, an examination of which will enable us to understand why liberalization simply made the country more vulnerable, leading to the crisis. This in turn could alert policy makers to the need to take some precautionary measures when advocating intervention in the functioning of the financial market and perhaps may enable them to strike a balance between intervention and the free market.

Accordingly, this chapter has been divided into two sections. In the first section we investigate why it is necessary to intervene and the nature of the intervention adopted by the South Korean government. However in order to investigate this issue, first we need to investigate the problems faced by developing countries in general, not from today's perspective, but from when these countries achieved their independence. In the second section we investigate what went wrong with the intervention and why.

5.2   AN ANALYSIS OF WHY INTERVENTION IS NECESSARY AND THE FORM IT COULD TAKE

Intervention will take the form of some regulations in order to protect depositors' funds, and also some other forms of intervention often will be required for the allocation of funds to ensure that certain sections of the community are not being deprived of access to the loan market. However, the level of intervention and the nature of intervention that will be required for developing countries will differ considerably from the type of intervention that is normally required for developed nations.

In order to understand why this is so, we will now examine the problems faced by developing countries when they achieved independence. Their economies then were described as being in a backward state, with high poverty, low education, high mortality rates, and so on. It was recognized that in their current state they could not escape from these problems, and nor did there exist any internal mechanism which indicated that this state was likely to change by itself in the near future. Yet in order to address these problems, it was essential to transform these economies from their backward state to an advanced industrial state without necessarily following the evolutionary stages that already-developed nations underwent. But this involved changing the structure of the economy from one state to another, where the principal aim was to improve the economic well-being of every member of the society. The ultimate objective of development is therefore to expand the existing entitlement set, especially for those who otherwise would remain in a deprived state.[2] Thus it is a conscious effort. It is this situation that will allow us to understand why the nature, and the levels, of intervention differ considerably from those experienced in the context of developed countries. But before we enter into an investigation of the nature and level of intervention, first we need to recognize a significant complication of the problems that are involved in the process of transferring the economy from one state to another.

The problem of developing countries in transferring the economy from one state to another is most succinctly described by Nurkse (1953), Rosenstein-Rodan (1943) and Scitovsky (1954). It was recognized from Kuznets' (1955) work that the process of development requires a higher accumulation of capital. But there was a problem in the process of capital accumulation, arising from both the supply side as well as the demand side. The supply problem principally arose from the low per capita income, which itself prevented the generation of sufficient savings that are required to increase the stocks of reproducible capital (Nurkse, 1953). The demand problem in capital formation also arose from the low per capita income, where the greater proportion of income went on necessities, leaving little to spend on industrial products. Consequently, the demand for industrial products remained low, causing a lack of incentive for private investors to invest in such industries. This problem was further exacerbated by the fact that the production process in modern industries represents complex sets of interdependent relationships among firms. In this situation, if the coordination among firms is to be propelled by the price-guided system, then investment in a firm may give rise to pecuniary external economies, and consequently its private profitability will understate its social desirability (Rosenstein-Rodan, 1943 and Scitovsky, 1954). This possibility of externalities arising from the intertemporal dependence among firms presented a serious impediment to the growth of developing countries.[3]

These problems particularly arise in multilinkage industries, where, in the absence of simultaneous growth, in the interdependent industries, one industry may not adjust to the growth in another industry due to difficulties in achieving economies of scale. The fact that these problems are particularly acute for developing countries principally arises not only from the deficiency in overall demand, but also from the further complication of an unequal distribution of income and wealth, causing difficulty in capturing the right pattern of demand. The central problem in multilinkage industries is whether a complementary decision will be made or not. This has a direct bearing on the future market, and whether the product will be sold. In other words, it is recognized that the investment decision involves undertaking some risk and uncertainty, where uncertainty principally arises from the fact that in these conditions investors are unable to approximate the future demand.[4] Furthermore, Scitovsky argues that private return is an imperfect indicator of social return.[5]

Thus, while Rosenstein-Rodan and Scitovsky point out the important impediments to development by identifying some of the exogeneous factors, from Solow's (1957) work we can recognize that the process of development is a much more complex issue than that which can be fully comprehended from the earlier writings of the authors mentioned above. The latter only concentrates on the exogeneous factors that present an impediment to growth, hence overlooking the importance of endogeneous factors that also stand as a barrier to development.

Solow's (1957) work suggests that technical progress plays a much greater role in the context of growth than savings. This therefore suggests that in the process of growth, one needs to address not only the exogeneous factors, but also the endogeneous factors, for which one needs to develop economic organizations whose principal task will be to address micro level issues. These organizations will play the role of information gathering and dissemination of information, and assist firms and industries in the more efficient utilization of productive resources over time.

It is recognized that the process of development does not just involve how to mobilize savings and how to eradicate deficiency in demand, but there is also the necessity to address a complex set of processes of learning how to operate newly created production facilities to cope with a changing structure of production.[6] These all involve development of a new set of institutions, whose principal task is to provide support to firms in exchange-related activities, such as marketing, communications, transport, the transfer of technology, credit and insurance. Thus the principal aim of these institutions is to remove the externalities that exist in the information processing and other exchange-related activities, and also to provide economies of scale and scope in these activities.[7]

Thus the process of development involves the mobilization of savings, channelling these savings into the most productive sectors of the economy, and in the presence of deficient demand, inducing firms to undertake projects which not only provide private returns but are also accompanied by a social return. In addition, development also involves the dissemination of information about new opportunities and new technology, and how to use them. While various informational and learning problems can be overcome by establishing specific types of institutions,[8] the mobilization of savings and the allocation of credit have to be carried out by banks. This means intervention will not only be required to develop the real sector, but will also be required in the financial sector to assist the development of the real sector. Here banks have a very important role to play.

Banks are profit-seeking organizations just like any other business. Their principal task is to raise deposits by offering interest, to re-lend these deposits to borrowers in the form of credit at a higher interest rate, and to make a profit from the difference between the loan rate and the deposit rate. Accordingly, any borrower who can meet a bank's credit standard requirements and promises to pay the interest rate, will obtain a loan. Should the borrower fail to meet his/her obligations, banks will resort to the credit standard. As long as these borrowers agree to repay the principal plus the interest rate and meet the banks' collateral requirements, they will receive loans. Banks as profit-seeking organizations are not concerned with whether these borrowers are using their loanable funds for productive or unproductive purposes, nor with whether the project for which the borrower seeks a loan, produces any social return or not.[9]

The above argument therefore suggests that the development process will require a change in the bankers' culture, that is, they will be required not only to investigate borrowers' credit worthiness, but also to assess the merits of borrowers' projects, not only in terms of their expected private rates of return but also in terms of their social rates of return.

Banks, in the early stages of the independence of developing countries, were engaged in advancing loans for trade-oriented activities and meeting working capital requirements. They were advancing loans for short-term purposes, but the process of development requires long-term and large loans. The size of operation of the majority of these banks was small, most of their dealings with short-term loans comprised smaller sized loans, and their survival depended upon short-term returns. Thus they developed neither the capital nor the necessary skill that is required to assess the merits of projects which involve large long-term loans. In addition to this, the greater proportion of the money market was controlled by the informal credit market.

The first problem that any government of a developing country faces, is how to bring the informal credit market under the umbrella of the formal credit market, so that a greater proportion of savings can be brought into the orbit of the formal market. One option is to open a number of branch facilities not only in the metropolitan area but also outside it. But the problem is that opening branch facilities, especially outside the metropolitan area, is costly, and a private bank whose principal motivation is to make a profit is unlikely to participate in such a venture. In addition to this, banks may not have sufficient capital to open additional branch facilities. But in the absence of higher levels of savings, a country cannot finance its development programme. This means that, in order to mobilize a higher than current level of savings, at least in the early stages of development, banks have to sacrifice certain levels of profit, but this should be a provisional measure and perhaps it is asking too much of a private bank.

Given the complex issues involved in the development process, the South Korean government adopted the path of export-led growth policy. The adoption of this policy allowed South Korea to avoid the problem that arises from internal demand deficiency. In fact, criticisms were often made of the Nurkse, Rosenstein-Rodan and Scitovsky model (Datta-Chowdhury, 1990), because it essentially concentrated on the internal demand condition when examining the problem of capital formation. This may be largely because of their own experience with stagnating trade in the first half of the 20th century. However, this changed dramatically in the 1950s. High growth rates in the OECD countries during the two decades following the Korean War led to a massive expansion in world trade. Rising wage rates in the developed countries also changed the pattern of the international division of labour, implying that poorer countries do not have to rely upon their internal markets to generate demand for capital formation. Furthermore, cold war tensions between the western nations and East European countries put South Korea in a very favourable position to take advantage of the export opportunities.

But the problem was that while government had to provide information about these opportunities to firms and to induce them to participate in such ventures, it also had to induce banks to participate. The government recognized that private banks were unlikely to participate in the promotion of export ventures and industry development programmes in their infancy because their markets were not established. In other words, whatever potential profit opportunities these markets offered, the future viability of these industries was not known to the banks. Furthermore, would-be participating firms in these markets often had neither an established track record as successful operators in these industries nor sufficient assets to offer as collateral to banks in order to obtain loans. As the government was the principal initiator of these programmes, it could not ask the participating privately owned firms to comply with the banks' credit standard requirements, especially when the firms themselves did not have sufficient information about these markets, a reason for which the government established the trading companies. Thus the South Korean government's second problem was how to induce private banks to participate in the development process.

The above argument suggests that successful implementation of the development strategy requires not only that banks increase their efforts to mobilize greater amounts of savings by offering a higher rate on deposits and by opening a larger number of branch facilities, but also that banks relax their credit standard requirements and offer cheaper credit facilities. Neither of these can be expected from private banks, since both strategies will result in a reduction in the banks' profit margin. At the same time banks would become more vulnerable in the event of borrowers' default, arising directly as a result of the reduction in the credit standard requirements and the reduction in the difference between loan rates and deposit rates. While the former implies that the banks would be carrying a higher credit risk, the latter implies that very few, if any, banks would be able to make provision for non-performing loans. The government recognized that, while the establishment of trading companies may provide support to producers in exchange-related activities, producers could not take advantage of the support that would be offered by these trading companies unless cheaper credit facilities could be provided.

5.3   WHERE INTERVENTION WENT WRONG

The complexities described above suggest that the implementation of such a policy would make the banks extremely fragile, and that this is similar to the situation that we observe when the financial system is liberalized. Therefore there is a need not only to undertake additional measures to ensure that the firms' reduction in revenue does not have a direct adverse impact on the banks' loan performance, but also to ensure a minimization of the banks' credit risk in the near future. Experience suggests that most governments have not recognized the fundamental weakness that emerges from this form of intervention. The South Korean government is no exception to this and therefore it also made no attempt to reduce the fragility of its banks. In order to highlight this issue, we will draw attention to three incidents, one of which is associated with the 1965 financial reform, the second with bailing out its troubled indebted firms in 1972, and the third with its restructuring of these firms in 1982.

In 1961 the South Korean government nationalized its major banks with the aim of establishing firm control over the financial system in order to execute the more effective mobilization of savings and to channel the savings to finance its five-year development plan. But neither the government nor its economic advisers recognized that having control over savings and allocation of credit does not give any control over the return on these financial assets. Therefore, undertaking a development programme whose financing requires a reduction in the banks' credit standard, means much of the banks' own performance will be largely interlocked with the performance of the projects for which they have advanced loans. In this situation, it is essential to ensure that the debt to equity ratio does not rise to a level where it will be difficult to make up any shortfall in the loan repayment that may arise as a result of the firm's loss of revenue due to demand deficiency, from the return on equity. Furthermore, the government needed to adopt two subsequent policies, one of which was to encourage these firms to develop an alternative pool of assets from the retention of their profits. This in turn would allow banks to take these alternative assets as collateral in the future, thereby unlocking the fate of the banks' loan capital from the performance of the indebted firms. The first policy, to be fully effective, would take a considerable number of years, and therefore the government needed to develop the second policy, which we refer to as intertemporal policy, which was to allow banks to monitor whether firms' production targets were in line with the demand for their output. At any point in time, if the supply of output exceeds its demand, then an unsold product will cause a reduction in the banks' earnings, and therefore it is often necessary to revise the production targets. It will be argued below, that of the three incidents mentioned above, two are largely the result of not undertaking these precautionary measures. In other words, neither the South Korean government, nor its advisers recognized that a relaxation of the credit standard is strictly a provisional measure. In fact, unprecedented growth in the loan capital was largely the result of not maintaining the credit standard, although it resulted in a high growth rate of GDP, but in the process, banks' loan capital was exposed to high credit risk. In other words, in the event of borrowers defaulting, a large portion of the banks' loan capital would not be recouped from the sale of collateral, and therefore bank failure would be inevitable.

The government brought the Bank of Korea (the Central) under the control of the Ministry of Finance and established several specialized banks. In order to raise the capital that was required to finance its development programme, the government actively sought foreign capital, and in addition, following the advice of the US aid mission team (Gurley, Patrick and Shaw, 1965), raised the interest rate on time deposits; which is often referred to as financial reform, and established new banks. The interest rate on time deposits was raised from 15 to 30 percent in 1965, and although this rate gradually declined, it remained above 20 percent up to 1971.[10] As a result of this high rate on deposits, the M2/GNP ratio rose from less than 9 percent to a little over 33 percent between 1964 and 1971.[11] This rapid growth of the formal financial sector was largely the result of high deposit rates, which induced asset holders to shift a portion of their funds from the informal credit market to banks. In other words, higher rates allowed the government to bring part of the savings that were kept in alternative forms, under the umbrella of nationalized banks. This higher rate also helped to increase the capital inflow, especially from Japan.

In order to provide cheaper credit facilities for its development programme, the government divided the loan portfolio into two groups. Export and infant industries formed one group and received a preferential loan rate of 6 percent and this rate remained below 10 percent up to 1980. The rest of the economy formed another group and received loans at a non-preferential rate. This rate rose from 16.9 percent to 26 percent between 1964 and 1965 and remained roughly around 24.4 percent between 1966 and 1970. By 1971 the rate had come down to 17 percent, and remained on average between 17 to 18 percent up to 1980.[12] In the absence of any other information, it appears that the preferential loans were subsidized by charging a very high rate on non-preferential loans. In this situation, a significant margin of difference should appear between the non-preferential loan rate and the rates on time deposits. But this was not the case. To begin with, between 1965 and 1968, rates on time deposits remained higher than those on non-preferential loans, implying that banks were running at a loss, independent of the project performance for which the banks advanced loans.[13] From 1969 the interest rate on non-preferential loans exceeded the interest rate on time deposits. But this was marginal, i.e. the interest rate on time deposits was 24 percent while the interest rate on non-preferential loans was 24.5. This margin of 0.5 percent was so small that perhaps it was only able to cover the administrative cost, and this margin hovered around 0.4 to 1 percent,[14] implying that no provisions were made for non-performing loans. The above fact suggests that the interest rate subsidization on preferential loans did not come from non-preferential loan rates. It then must have come directly from the government or from cheaper foreign capital. This suggests that the success of the 1965 financial reform was made at the cost of banks.[15]

Despite this higher interest rate on time deposits, domestic mobilization of savings was not sufficient to finance its investment expenditure, and as a result South Korea had to rely on foreign capital. However, this higher rate made foreign loans much cheaper than domestic loans, which in turn encouraged Korean borrowers to seek overseas loans.[16] Korea borrowed mainly to finance its balance of payment deficits and to finance its long-term investment programme and its foreign debt rose from US$206 million to US$2.922 billion, and the ratio of foreign debt/GNP rose from 7 percent to 30 percent between 1965 and 1971 (Amsden, 1989). With the government providing guarantees on foreign loan repayments, firms resorted to foreign loans in order to finance imports of capital goods that were required for the production of export items, and used the domestic loans in order to finance other exporting activities. As the economy grew, large firms, in order to maintain a high rate of investment, not only relied on foreign and domestic bank loans but often resorted to the informal credit market (i.e. the unregulated financial market) for short-term loans when the need arose. Initially this was not a problem when exports constituted only a small fraction (5–7 percent) of GNP, but when the share of exports exceeded 20 percent of GNP, the importance of the outflow of credit in the context of its inflationary impact was recognized.[17] But what was not recognized was that the magnitude of the problem was not confined only to the issue of inflation but had much wider ramifications for the financial system in the long run.

The fundamental problem with the Korean economy was that it was a debt financing investment growth economy. That is, as the economy grew, firms instead of gradually remitting past debts and placing a greater emphasis on internal funds to grow, placed a greater emphasis on external capital for their growth rate.[18] Initially, the problem with this form of financing growth was not recognized, mainly because as the economy grew, so did its ability to service the contractual debt commitment, all things being equal. This steady flow of return on loans in turn increased firms' credit ratings. Consequently, lenders' willingness to offer larger loans to these firms also increased.[19] With the increasing access to credit, investors (i.e. borrowers) also did not feel the necessity to rely on internal funds to any great extent for growth, and as a result their share of these funds in relation to total funds shrank. This in turn caused the debt/equity ratio to rise with the growth of the firm, thereby causing the debt service ratio to rise, which in turn, in the absence of an appropriate credit standard, exposed banks' capital to very high levels of credit risk. For example, as the share of exports rose from 5 to 7 percent in the mid 1960s to over 20 percent of GNP by the 1970s (Cole and Park, 1983), the firms' share of internal funds in relation to total funds shrank from 47.7 percent during 1963–65 to 25.4 percent during 1966–71, while the share of external funds rose from 52.3 percent to 74.6 percent (Amsden and Euh, 1993). During the same period, i.e. between 1963 and 1971, the debt/equity ratio rose from 92 to 328 percent and the debt service ratio as a percentage of merchandise exports rose from 5.20 to 28.34 percent (Amsden, 1989). The problem is that if the export earnings fall and, as a result, the rate of return from the total investment falls below the repayment rate on the debt commitment, the rate of return from the internal funds may not be sufficient to meet the shortfall. Firms then have to borrow in order to meet their debt commitments. South Korea faced this problem in 1972.

As the economy grew, the cost of production increased, and exporting firms started to face increasing difficulty in meeting the ever-rising export target. This problem was further magnified by the fact that there was a growing resistance from two of its main markets, namely Japan and the USA, to importing certain products, such as textiles, which in turn further slowed down the growth in export earnings. In order to rectify this problem the government devalued the currency with the hope that this would pick up the demand for the export industry. But the devaluation instead caused a corresponding rise in the cost of servicing the foreign loans, which further added to the total cost of servicing loans. The return from the equity (i.e. internal funds), which constituted only 25 percent of the total investment, was not sufficient to meet the shortfall. Firms had no option other than to borrow in order to meet their debt obligations.[20] Many large firms turned to the informal credit market in order to meet short-term cash shortages. An increasing number of firms found that they were unable to meet the principal and interest rate payments to their foreign creditors. By 1971, the number of bankrupt firms receiving foreign loans rose to 200 (Cho, 1989). As the banks neither imposed a credit standard when advancing loans to firms nor made any provision for non-performing loans, this suggests that the bankruptcy cost had to be borne by the banks. This means the depositors also had to incur a loss. On the other hand, as the government authorized every single foreign loan in order to keep firm control over the foreign capital inflow, now it had an obligation to honour these overseas debts. Furthermore, as South Korea never had sufficient domestic savings to achieve a high growth rate, it had to rely on overseas loans, and the government could not afford to default on foreign loans.

Following the advice of the indebted firms, the government in August 1972 declared the Presidential Emergency Decree, which gave power to the government to invalidate all the loan agreements between firms and informal credit lenders, and instituted a new agreement whereby lenders had the option to transfer the loans into shares in the borrowing firms.[21] Thus the 1972 Emergency Decree, which bailed out troubled firms, did so mainly at the cost of depositors with both the informal credit market and the banks. This desperate act might have allowed these firms to meet their overseas debt obligations, but for the fact that the government did not recognize that the problem might have emerged from over-investment. The possibility of over-investment particularly arises for the two following reasons: (a) a reduction in the credit standard allows borrowers to borrow more than they would be able to borrow if the normal credit standard requirements were implemented; (b) a reduction in the credit standard requirements may encourage firms to borrow more, since the borrowers know that the higher the credit risk, the greater the likelihood that lenders would organize a rescue package in the event of an adverse performance of the project. This possibility of organizing the rescue package may make the borrower indifferent to risk, or what is popularly referred to as the possible source of moral hazard.[22] Of course it depends what fraction of the lender's total wealth has been tied to such a project. In fact, the limit on a bank loan that a given firm can obtain, when determined by the credit standard requirements, itself prevents firms from undertaking over-investment. This is because the firm knows that in the event of an unsuccessful venture it has much to lose, since its income from other assets will be used to repay the loans.

However, it was recognized that in the early stages of development often it is not possible to maintain the credit standard requirements, and in this situation it was essential to ensure that entrepreneurial capital constituted a larger share in the investment projects. This in turn would have ensured that in the event of an unsuccessful venture a reduction in the entrepreneurs' income would not prevent them from maintaining their loan repayment. Nevertheless, one would imagine that one learns from one's own mistakes, but experience suggests that this did not make the government more prudent in its lending policy. It neither encouraged firms to rely more on internal funds as opposed to external funds for their growth, nor allowed banks to make provision for non-performing loans and to introduce credit standard requirements. Instead, the government embarked on its next expensive project.

In the 1970s, the government decided to develop heavy and chemical industries. It appears that this decision was principally due to the fact that despite its high growth performance in the export-oriented sector, South Korea's reliance on imported inputs for the production of export items remained high. As a result, from every dollar it earned from the sale of its export items, 67 cents went to pay Japanese import bills (Chakravarty, 1987a). The combined impact of this import bill in addition to its reliance on overseas capital did not ease South Korea's foreign debt problem, despite its high performance in the export sector.[23] Consequently, it was necessary for South Korea to attempt to reduce its reliance on imported inputs. But this venture was so risky that even many large firms were reluctant to embark on such a project. This is largely because of the fact that the development of these new industries required very extensive investment in fixed capital and technology, with a long lag and an uncertain return. Furthermore, it was not clear whether the export market was sufficiently large to allow these industries to achieve economies of scale, thus meaning that it too had to capture new markets. Given the difficulties, the government used a similar method that it had used in the past to encourage firms to enter into priority industries, which was to offer a strong package of tax and financial incentives to encourage some of the largest firms with minimum equity to enter into them. In addition to these incentives, the government introduced local content regulations and these also applied to the export sector.[24]

Throughout the 1970s the output of heavy and chemical industries grew rapidly. Their share in the export market also grew rapidly, but it was not sufficient to achieve economies of scale. By the late 1970s these industries were carrying a substantial amount of excess capacity, and coupled with the collapse of foreign markets in construction, shipping and shipbuilding in the early 1980s, the GNP turned negative for the first time since the Korean War. As the share of internal funds in relation to the total investment was not sufficient to meet the shortfall that arose in their debt commitment, firms started to borrow again in order to meet this shortfall. As a result, their share of internal funds shrank from an average of 21.1 percent during 1975–79 to 16.4 percent by 1980, while their share of external funds rose from 78.9 percent to 83.6 percent (Choong-Hwan, 1990). The debt/equity ratio rose from around 370 percent during the late 1970s to 488 percent by 1980 and as a result of this heavy borrowing Korea's external debt as a percentage of GNP rose from 32 percent to 48 percent between 1979 and 1981 (Amsden, 1989). By 1982, a growing number of highly indebted firms found it difficult to service their debt. The South Korean government once again was forced to assist in restructuring industrial firms that faced financial difficulties. Thus the problem of 1971 repeated itself, that is, the problem of over-investment.

It appears that the South Korean government failed to recognize that this likelihood of over-investment periodically emerges in the absence of credit standard requirements, especially when firms' own share of capital, in relation to the size of the investment, is small. Thus it was essential for the government to introduce credit standard requirements, but it neither addressed this issue nor attempted to increase firms' share of internal capital as opposed to external capital. Instead, preferential lending rates were eliminated in 1982, and the government decided to abstain from further directed credit programmes. In addition, NBFI were further deregulated and corporations were allowed to issue bonds with a guarantee by commercial banks. The government privatized the commercial banks, but in the presence of large non-performing loans, could not abstain from maintaining its control over the banking sector, as the restructuring of the industrial sector required government supervision of credit allocation. The government maintained its control over the interest rate and the credit allocation of the banking sector, which was fully lifted in 1991, along with its control over the foreign capital inflow. But the external share as opposed to the internal share of the total investment remained very high. In fact during 1987–91, the share of external funds constituted 73.6 percent, while the internal share constituted merely 26.4 percent, of the total investment (Amsden and Euh, 1993). Thus the banking sector remained over-exposed. By 1994, banks had to increase their allocated funds in order to make provision for bad loans,[25] but there exists no evidence to suggest that the government made any systematic attempt to reduce the debt/equity ratio. For example, even in 1996 the average debt to equity ratio for the top 30 Chaebol was 898.49 percent. This means these firms borrowed an average of 8.98 dollars against each dollar they owned, and the greater proportion of the loans either came directly from the banks, or was raised via issuing corporate bonds, which were also guaranteed by the banks. Fourteen of these 30 Chaebol were making a negative profit in 1996, while for those who were making a positive profit, this remained marginal compared with the total assets, including loans, that were invested (Lee, 1997).

Thus it was only a matter of time before these firms' aggressive unsuccessful ventures would lead to massive bank failures.

5.4 CONCLUSION

The problem for developing countries is that, to undertake certain projects it is often necessary to reduce the banks' credit standard requirements, otherwise those projects would not be undertaken. In these cases, the government then becomes the risk bearer in order to protect the banks. But it is important for the government to recognize that in this situation the banking sector becomes fragile. Unfortunately, it is the latter factor which often has not been recognized, as in the case of South Korea. In fact, South Korea's high growth rate was largely due to growth in loan capital, but in the process it made its banking sector extremely fragile, and this was overlooked. Throughout its 30 years of unprecedented growth, South Korea's banking sector remained fragile. Between 1965 and 1968 it was running at a loss. In 1972, banks again made a loss, and this in particular came about because banks were neither allowed to introduce credit standard requirements nor to make provisions for non-performing loans. Despite this experience, the government made no attempt to rectify the situation, and thus the problem appeared again in 1982. This time it undertook various reforms, which the World Bank referred to as a 'market friendly approach'. They comprised various deregulatory measures, but did not address the issue of the banks' fragility. Thus when total deregulation came in 1991, the South Korean banks were highly exposed to credit risk, without government backing. As shown, even in 1996, large corporations' debt/equity ratio was extremely high, and profit levels were very low and a little less than half of these firms were making losses. This fact suggests that a number of firms were having problems maintaining their debt payment obligations in 1996; thus, as this problem increased, a banking crisis was inevitable. In fact, as some commentators argue, the annual growth rate of 8.2 percent between 1962 and 1982 was largely attributed to foreign capital, in the absence of which the growth rate would have been in the magnitude of 4.9 percent (Vittas and Cho, 1996). Although the latter statement is a matter of guesswork, there is no doubt that foreign capital played a very important role. Most importantly, its high risk credit policy and appropriate economic organization might have produced such a high growth rate, but it is the high risk credit policy that ultimately brought about the banking crisis.[26]

NOTES

1. This literature follows from the asymmetric information constraint which may cause market failure and as a result it is argued that intervention will be necessary. See Stiglitz (1993), Gertler and Rose (1994) and Hellmann *et al.* (2000) for further details. Even the World Bank's (1993) report agrees 'mild' repression may be beneficial.

2. It is important to recognize that development and growth are not the same thing, as the latter is a prerequisite for the former, where the former involves improving the economic well-being of every member of the society. See Streeten (1981) and Sen (1983) on this issue. Unfortunately, the school of liberalization does not recognize the importance of this distinction, and this may be largely because of the fact that the model they use to promote their view, is based on the assumption that everyone starts with equal endowments. Observation reveals that such an assumption is simply not a reflection of reality.

3. Even in modern corporations which are mostly vertically integrated, inter-plant coordinations are not guided by the price system, but rather are based on a response to needs as they become apparent. Now we shall elaborate on this issue briefly. Suppose the price of rice increases, which provides a signal to the farmers that there is a higher demand for rice. This leads farmers to increase their per unit land output, and this will tend to lead to a fall in the price of rice. Assume fertilizer is the only variable input that is required for the production of rice. Thus the decision by the farmers to increase production will in turn cause a rise in demand for fertilizer, thereby leading to a rise in the price of fertilizer. This provides a signal to the fertilizer producers that there is a higher demand, and therefore they should increase the productive capacity of the fertilizer plant. The problem is that fertilizer producers are not sure whether the additional productive facility will allow them to achieve economies of scale. This problem arises from the two following facts: (a) price may give a signal that there is a higher demand, but this signal does not specify the actual size of the demand. Thus installing an additional productive facility, in the absence of knowledge in relation to the actual demand, may cause a firm to run at excess capacity. This problem particularly arises because the productive capacity of a facility is given, and therefore when the actual demand falls short of the expected demand, then the firm can adjust its output but cannot eliminate excess capacity. The cost of this excess capacity in fact then may reduce a firm's profitability. (b) There is non-symmetric distribution of land and wealth among farmers, which causes not only a variation in their purchasing ability, but also a variation in their access to the credit market. This in turn causes a problem for the producers to estimate the effective demand, not the potential demand. In this situation, price may provide a signal, but due to the existence of (a) and (b), a firm may not respond to such a signal, since the latter does not say anything about (a) and (b), thereby giving rise to externalities. In this situation, government intervention will be required. These issues have been exhaustively discussed in the context of Planning Models. For further details see Rudra (1975).

4. See Chakravarty (1993a) for further details on this issue.

5. See Sen (1984b) on this issue although it is discussed in a different context.

6. See Arrow (1962) on this issue, where he explains how worker productivity increases over time as they acquire skills. See also Haavelmo (1954) who emphasizes the role of education, Kaldor (1961) on the technical progress function and Romer (1990) who introduces learning and technical change. Without going into the intricate arguments of the above authors, the main theme of their contribution can be summarized with a brief example that is drawn from the experience of Indian farmers during the

introductory period of the green revolution, which shows that technical change, education and learning by doing, all played an important role in improving productivity. The High Yielding Variety (HYV) of seeds itself is a technical breakthrough in the cultivation of rice, wheat or maize, as it offers a higher output per unit of land, compared with the local variety. These seeds were originally developed in the Wheat and Maize Institute in Mexico and the International Rice Research Institute in the Philippines. But the problem was, farmers in India did not know about this progress, nor did they know that the use of these seeds required some additional knowledge over and above that acquired in the process of local variety cultivation. The Indian government used various means to disseminate this information to the farmers about the benefits of this variety and to educate them about how to use these seeds. Radio broadcasting was one of the most effective means that was used during this period. Other means of learning came directly from learning by doing. In other words, farmers learned during the process of cultivation through experience. Let us briefly elaborate on this issue with an example. These varieties have certain requirements and features which distinguish them from the local variety; such as, they require an assured and controlled water supply with higher doses of fertilizer, they have a shorter maturity period and they have a shorter height. Where tubewell facilities were not readily available, farmers initially planted HYV rice seeds in low lying fields, in order to ensure that they received adequate water. Low lying fields are generally situated in the middle of paddy fields. HYV's shorter maturity period compared with the local variety was known to farmers. They knew from their experience that during harvesting birds attack the paddy field and they used to take measures in an attempt to deter them. But what they did not know was the intense impact of all these birds concentrating their attack on a small plot of land compared with an attack that was dispersed over the entire field. Farmers lost their entire crop in that plot as a result of this concentrated attack, neither being able to harvest it quickly nor to transport the harvested crop, as this involved crossing fields where the local variety was planted. Since then farmers have never planted HYV beside the local variety. The second thing they learned from experience is that HYV requires adequate drainage. During the heavy monsoon season often the water covered the local variety, which can survive under water for a few days, which in turn gives adequate time for the farmers to drain the water out. However the HYV's shorter height meant the water covered it even in the early period of the heavy monsoon, and its low resistance power, compared with that of the local variety, for surviving under water, meant that this combination of circumstances would destroy the entire crop. These facts were not known in advance of their occurrence, and farmers acquired this knowledge through experience during the process of cultivation. This therefore may suggest that some endogeneous factors play an important role in increasing the rate of growth of output: the first is the technical breakthrough (which could be exogeneous or endogeneous) in the method of production, the second is education and the third is learning by doing. Institutions play an extremely important role in providing the first two, while the third comes through experience. Needless to say, despite any negative points the green revolution may have had, its success in terms of higher output would never have taken place without government intervention in the agriculture production method.

7.　For further details on this issue see Datta-Chaudhuri (1990) and Lall (1994).

8.　South Korea was particularly successful in developing various trading companies, which provided many exchange-related facilities. These institutions are largely responsible for the high growth performance. See Jones and Sakong (1980), Amsden (1989), Westphal (1990), Datta-Chaudhuri (1990), Lall (1994) and Singh (1994) for further details on this issue.

9.　As pointed out in the previous section, under the free market mechanism there will be a tendency for the loan capital to move away from the productive aspect of the economy in favour of financial assets, where investors acquire these assets with the expectation that they will be making a positive gain on future changes in the price of these assets. It is this form of activity which we refer to as unproductive. As pointed out in Chapter 1, in the United States following the Great Depression, an act was introduced to prevent such movement in 1934. Similarly, in 1946 in the UK an act was introduced in order to ensure that such movement would not starve the industrial sector of loan capital. See Sayers (1960a) for further details on this issue. Similarly, in the third world countries many traders used to purchase agricultural products such as rice, wheat, maize, oil seeds etc. just after the harvest when the price was low and release them just before the harvesting season when the price of these products was high. Here also they were making a gain from the expected changes in the price of these products. In order to prevent these unproductive activities the Indian government, as will be discussed in the next chapter, introduced an act which restricted banks from advancing loans for such purposes; furthermore they also introduced food procurement programmes.

10. See Amsden (1989) and Cho (1989).
11. See Cole and Park (1983). See also Cho (1989) and Kim (1991) on the above issue. However Amsden (1989) pointed out that although household savings as a percentage of GNP increased from 0.18 percent in 1965 to 4.15 percent in 1966, it declined in the following year. From then onwards no systematic relationship can be observed between interest rate and saving behaviour. This may emphasize the point that was made in Chapter 4 section 4.2, i.e. higher interest rates mainly assist in the mobilization of savings.
12. See Cho (1989), Amsden (1989) and Amsden and Euh (1993).
13. For example, the tables that we have consulted from the authors (Cho, 1989; Amsden, 1989 and Amsden and Euh, 1993) indeed suggest that the interest rate on time deposits remained higher than the rate on non-preferential loans between 1965 and 1968. In the absence of any other information this suggests that banks were running at a loss during these four years. However, none of the authors make any comment on this disparity between the rates on non-preferential loans and deposit rates. On the other hand, Cole and Park (1983) point out that this higher rate of between 24 to 28 percent per annum on regular commercial loans, which remained below the rate paid on the time deposits of more than one year of maturity, or in other words, this reverse margin, attracted criticism from the banking community.
14. See Cho (1989).
15. That is unless we would like to assume that the banks invested part of the deposits in the unregulated financial market, since the interest rate on loans in this sector was higher than the rate on time deposits.
16. On average there was 12.9 percent difference between Korean loans and foreign loans (i.e. from the US and Japan) during the period from 1966–70 (Amsden, 1989). See also Park (1985) who pointed out that between 1965 and 1970, the divergence between domestic and foreign borrowing rates ranged from 4.4 percent to 18 percent.
17. See Cole and Park (1983) on this issue.
18. In the absence of a well-developed stock market, in developing countries external capital mainly comes from the banks and other NBFI.
19. Experience in the last 20 years of a larger number of banking crises in developing countries than in developed countries indicates that this willingness is perhaps greater in the former than in the latter. This difference in willingness between the two categories of nations may have emerged due to the gap in experience in that one achieved through an evolutionary process while the other was too young and yet had to go through the necessary preliminaries that are involved in the process of development.

20. This problem can be more clearly observed from Choong-Hwan (1990), who presents figures for the internal and external share of funds for the periods 1963–69 and 1970–74, which show that while in the former period this on average was 33.3 and 66.7 percent respectively, for the latter period it changed to 25.7 and 74.3 respectively. This shows that as the economy slowed down, firms started to have difficulty in meeting their debt commitment, and in order to meet this commitment they resorted to borrowing and as a result further reduced their share of internal funds.

21. For further details see Bank of Korea (1973), Cole and Park (1983), Amsden (1989) and Cho (1989).

22. This is an issue which has been exhaustively discussed within the game theory framework in various contexts. See Jensen and Meckling (1976), Stiglitz and Weiss (1981), De Meza and Webb (1987) and Gertler (1992).

23. Once the economy accumulates an excessive debt, there is a need to improve the labour productivity, since relying entirely on exports exceeding imports and a higher marginal propensity to save may not be sufficient to remit its debt obligation. See Bhaduri (1987) on this complicated issue.

24. For further details see Cole and Park (1983) and Westphal (1990).

25. See Bank of Korea (1994).

26. Of course, following the financial crisis, various opinions have been expressed as to its cause, e.g. cronyism (Wade, 1998), panic (Radelet and Sachs, 1998), and so on. For a comprehensive summary and criticism of these views see Arestis and Glickman (2002). These two authors, using Minsky's financial instability hypothesis, show that financial liberalization will lead to financial fragility.

6. Intervention II: The Indian experience

6.1 INTRODUCTION

The Indian government also intervened in the real sector as well as in the financial sector in order to develop the nation in a similar way to the South Korean government. The reason for the intervention was the same as that described in the previous chapter, and the level of intervention was also comparable to that of the South Korean government. Both countries adopted a five year planning model in order to develop their respective nations. While both countries' objectives were the same, however, there was a significant difference in the paths they pursued in order to achieve their respective objectives. While South Korea followed the path of an export-led growth strategy,[1] India on the other hand adopted an import substitution policy for its development.[2] This caused the two economies to differ in a very important way in terms of the priorities they had in place in order to develop their respective nations, and consequently both derived very different results. Adoption of an export-led growth strategy allows a country to avoid the problem of uncertainty (or inadequate market) that arises from the possibility of internal demand deficiency, which in turn arises from the existence of a high poverty rate, as pointed out by Rosenstein-Rodan, Scitovsky and other development theorists. This means the country does not have to address the issue of poverty simultaneously with the issue of industrialization, and industry can achieve economies of scale quickly without addressing the poverty directly, provided it can capture a sufficient share of the export market.

Compared with this model, countries such as India, which adopted the policy of import substitution, could not avoid the problem of uncertainty that arises from the possibility of demand deficiency and this meant it had to address the issue of poverty simultaneously with the issue of industrialization. This added to the complexity of the problem, which here was twofold. Firstly, the government had to directly address how to reduce the level of poverty, so that the standard of living could be raised to a level which could adequately address the problem of demand deficiency. Secondly, it had to plan for industrialization in a manner that could take care of the problem of internal demand deficiency. This meant the nation's scarce resources[3] would be divided into two parts, one of which would be spent directly on addressing the issue of poverty and the other on industrialization. Thus the expected growth rate would be lower than that of countries which adopted an export-led growth strategy, at least in the early stages of development.

This analysis suggests that although the level of intervention by the two respective governments may have been the same, there was a subtle difference in the kind of intervention required in the case of India. In South Korea, the government selected the priority sectors according to their export opportunities. Thus the government's job as far as finance was concerned was to organize the finance to these sectors, including its supporting sectors. As mentioned above, the case of India was much more complex, as the government had to organize the finance not only to promote industry, but also to address the issue of demand deficiency. Hence, it had to address the issue of poverty. As around 80 percent of the population's livelihood directly and indirectly depended on agriculture, the government had to organize loans for this section of the community in order to improve their living standard. This meant government also had to induce banks to open branch facilities in the rural areas. In addition to this, loans had to be organized for artisans and small businesses. A complication of the problem arises here. Owing to its inaccessibility to any formal loan market facility, this sector formed an alternative loan market, the operational characteristics of which were not known much to the government. Fragmented information that was available at the time only revealed its exploitative operational characteristics. Thus there was an urgent need for the government to organize bank loan facilities to this sector. It faced two critical problems in order to organize loans for poor people. The first was associated with the fact that poor people do not have tangible assets that are readily recognized by banks as collateral, and thus the problem was how to meet banks' credit standards. The second problem was that as the size of the loans on these occasions would be small, the administrative cost per unit of loan would be high compared with larger loans. Thus given the interest rate, these loans would be less profitable than their larger counterparts. The issue therefore was how the government could induce commercial banks to offer loans to these groups of borrowers.

Given the complexity of the problems described above, this chapter is divided into two sections. In the first section, we will investigate why government decided to intervene, with reference to India. In the second section, we will investigate what can go wrong and why. This will be followed by policy suggestions.

6.2 THE INDIAN GOVERNMENT'S REASONS FOR INTERVENTION AND ITS CONSEQUENCES

The commercial banks that were operating in the early 1950s mainly advanced loans to the trade-oriented part of the economy and specialized in the provision of short-term or working capital loans, mostly in the form of cash-credit and overdraft facilities (against the hypothecation of marketable tangible assets). They were mainly operating in urban and industrial locations, their size of operation was small, and therefore they had neither the means nor the willingness to extend the large and long-term loans that were necessary for industrial development. They were also reluctant to open branches to mobilize savings from, and to facilitate loans to, the rural areas. Small scale enterprises could not qualify to obtain loans from these banks. Their principal clients were large industrial houses, wholesale traders and a very few rich landowners.

In fact, a large part of the country's economic activity mostly relied on a highly unorganized fragmented credit market for loans. These lenders also offered loans of a smaller size for short-term purposes against collateral whose value often exceeded the value of the principal. Their interest rates were higher than the rates charged by the banking sector and they offered loans mainly for consumption purposes and to meet borrowers' working capital requirements. Thus neither the organized nor the unorganized money markets were equipped to offer the kind of facilities that were required for the nation's development. The market can be perceived as being relatively free during this period, in the sense of not being subjected to undue intervention by the government. But the banks in their existing form were not equipped to mobilize the level of savings that was necessary for financing the kind of projects the country needed. Therefore, there was the need for intervention to equip the banks to adequately address the above issues.[4]

The necessity for intervention arose not only in order to mobilize a higher level of savings, but also to channel savings into the industrial sector, agriculture, small businesses and artisans. To mobilize a higher level of savings, there is a need to tap the savings that otherwise remain in alternative forms. To do that, the interest rate on deposits has to be increased and, in addition, banks' branch facilities have to be extended outside the metropolitan areas. The latter is also required to facilitate loans to the agricultural sector. Furthermore, to develop the industrial sector, there is a need to organize large long-term loans and, at the same time, in order to develop the agricultural sector and address the poverty, there is a need to make provision for a large number of smaller loans for agriculture, small businesses and artisans. Accordingly, the Indian government's intervention concentrated on three areas of the loan market. Firstly, it intervened in order to mobilize a higher level of savings to finance its development programme. Secondly, it intervened in order to channel a greater amount of loanable funds to the socially more productive areas of the economy. Thirdly, it intervened in order to improve the smaller and marginal borrowers' access to the loan market.

The first area of intervention worked out well for India. It involved encouraging banks to merge with other competing banks, so they would have a sufficient capital base to finance the extension of branch facilities outside the metropolitan area. This would give a greater opportunity for banks to mobilize a higher level of savings than that which prevailed at that time. In addition, this higher level of savings would allow the government and investors to undertake large long-term investment projects and also to allocate credit to the agricultural sector, small businesses and artisans. Banks merged with other banks, either voluntarily or as a result of the Reserve Bank of India's (RBI) advice, and the total number decreased from 605 to 85 between 1950 and 1969. Bank branches increased from 4151 to 8262, the population per bank branch decreased from 97,000 to 65,000 and GDS as a percentage of GDP rose from 10.2 to 15.7 percent during the same period (Krishnaswamy et al., 1987). However, it is important to note that the government had significant difficulty in inducing banks to open branch facilities in the rural areas. Private banks remained reluctant to participate in such a scheme, and thus in the early days most of these branch facilities were extended via government sponsored banks such as Cooperatives, Land Mortgage Banks and the State Bank of India (SBI).[5] In fact, in 1969 only 22.2 percent of the banks' total branch facilities were located in the rural areas.

However, the banks' performance, both in terms of the extension of branch facilities outside the metropolitan areas as well as in terms of mobilizing savings, was impressive following their nationalization in

1969. Between 1969 and 1985, branch numbers increased from 8262 to 48,930, and the population per branch decreased from 65,000 to 14,000. By 1985, 57.5 percent of the branches were operating in the rural area and a further 19.5 percent in the semi-urban area (which means they were located predominantly outside the metropolitan centres and large towns). As a result of these extensions, there was a massive rise in the number of depositors, resulting in a further rise in GDS from 15.7 to 24 percent of GDP between 1969 and 1985. By 1980, over 92 percent of total deposits came under the control of public sector banks. By the middle of 1985, commercial bank deposits amounted to Rs. 764 billion, which was 67 percent more than at the end of 1981 (Krishnaswamy *et al.*, 1987). The population per branch remained 14,000 in 1993, deposits as a percentage of national income rose from 15.3 to 51.8 between 1969 and 1994, and the share of the total deposits for the rural population increased from 7.2 to 14.6 percent between 1973 and 1993 (Sen and Vaidya, 1997).

Thus the objective of greater mobilization of savings was met largely as a result of the extension of bank branch facilities, and the banks' performance at face value was quite impressive in this area of intervention. But when one considers the cost of mobilization, their performance would not appear to be as impressive as the figures on mobilization might suggest, as most of these deposits were small in size, and as a result the administrative cost per unit of deposit would be expected to increase to a very high level. Thus, overall, the operating costs of banks would be expected to increase as a result of the extension of branch facilities.[6] The question therefore needs to be investigated whether the return from the loans could compensate for this high operating cost.

When considering the allocation of loans for the socially more productive areas of the economy and for the improvement of smaller and marginal borrowers' access to the loan market, intervention was less successful from the very beginning. This is equally true in terms of the return on loans. Initially, it was thought that much of the banks' credit could be channelled into the socially more productive areas of the economy via the RBI's regulations and incentives. The remainder of the credit facilities could then be provided via the development of financial corporations and government sponsored banks, such as the Industrial Finance Corporations (IFC), Industrial Development Bank of India (IDBI), Cooperative Banks and Land Mortgage Banks, and to provide assistance to small scale enterprises similar institutions were developed.[7] Both the IFC and IDBI were originally established in order to organize the large long-term loans that were required for the industrial sector's development. IFC and IDBI clients in general are large borrowers, and no significant problem was reported or observed in relation to their ability either to raise large long-term capital or to meet large working capital requirements from the banks.[8] But the problem arose in the government's effort to divert credit to agriculture and small scale enterprises, where the RBI's regulations and incentives largely remained ineffective. It was noted that much of the banks' credit was still being received by private traders, especially wholesale traders and large entrepreneurs. Wholesale traders used this credit for the purchase of foodgrains, edible oils, oil seeds, raw cotton, sugar etc., with the expectation that they would make a gain from future changes in the prices of these items.[9] In the case of industry, the banks' finance mainly went to maintain inventories and left the entrepreneurs to use their own retained earnings or else to seek loans from other financial institutions to finance their fixed investments.

This led the RBI to further tighten up its regulatory devices over banks' operations. It introduced various selective credit controls, such as regulations against loans for the purchase of foodgrains, edible oils, oil seeds, raw cotton, sugar etc, in anticipation that they might force banks to divert their credit facilities from the wholesale traders. In addition, it also introduced an upper limit on the size of loan that otherwise might be obtained by any individual borrower as a working capital loan, known as the Credit Authorization Scheme (CAS) in 1965. This scheme stated that any private borrower wishing to borrow Rs. 10 million and over, required official approval from the RBI.[10] At the same time, in order to improve the access of small-scale enterprises, and agriculture and export-oriented activities to the banks' credit, the RBI offered various incentives, including a scheme for guaranteeing bank credit to small-scale sectors, with specific incentives to promote particular types of advances. For example, to promote engineering exports, it provided refinance against packing or post-shipment credit to exporters at the low rate of 4.5 percent, with the agreement that the banks' lending rates on those loans should not exceed 6 percent per annum. Extensive lending support was also provided by the RBI in the form of contributions to the Agricultural Refinance Corporation. Despite these measures, credit still went to those who had larger assets, and the government was unable to improve smaller and marginal borrowers' access to the loan market. While the share of credit favouring industry rose from 34 to 67.5 percent, bank credit to the agricultural sector merely rose from 1.1 to 2 percent of the total credit between 1951 and 1968 (Gupta, 1988).[11] But to address poverty, the agricultural sector required a much higher share of the total credit and this requirement was further increased by the mid-1960s.

By the mid-1960s the Indian government had adopted the High Yielding Variety Programme (HYVP) in order to become self-sufficient in food production. This programme was adopted because HYV seeds offer a higher yield per unit of land than local varieties, but require higher doses of fertilizer and controlled irrigational facilities. This means the cost of cultivation when using HYV seed is much higher than when using local varieties. This increases the need to make greater provision for further credit facilities to agriculture. The government recognized that the government-sponsored banks alone would not be able to extend the loan facilities that were required for the successful implementation of the HYVP and to address the growing income disparity, which was rising rapidly between the urban and the rural population. The private banks' reluctance to extend loan facilities outside the metropolitan areas was known to the government. It was a widely held view then that the banks became an instrument to divert community savings to enhance the profits and economic power of the urban private sectors, thereby misallocating the nation's scarce resources that otherwise would have been invested in its development. The government decided that to serve essential social purposes these banks had to be nationalized, and in 1969 it nationalized the private banks.[12] This gave considerable power to the government over the banks. It then introduced 'lead banks schemes', under which a particular public sector bank was designated as the lead bank for a district, and its principal task was to investigate the credit requirements of that district, and to facilitate credit accordingly.

Furthermore, by 1972, the government adopted a number of poverty alleviation and employment generation schemes. It selected certain sectors of the economy, referred to as 'priority sectors' (which included agriculture and allied activities, small-scale industry, retail trade, transport operations, professionals and craftsmen/women) and decided that commercial banks must assist these sectors by facilitating cheap loans. In short, 'priority sectors' mainly comprised small businesses and agriculture. It was thought that the improvement in access to a cheaper loan facility by small businesses might generate higher employment, which itself would take care of part of the poverty. The remainder of the poverty was to be directly addressed by loan assistance schemes to the poor, as a result of which they could set up their own businesses, or at least would have reduced dependence on private moneylenders for loans at a higher interest rate. This in turn could allow them to retain much of their own surplus. This meant that part of the aim of this programme was that commercial bank loans must reach the tiniest units of the economy. Accordingly, the government declared that by March 1979, 'priority sectors' as a whole must receive 33 percent of the total bank credit. A little less than 50 percent of this was allocated to the agricultural sector, amounting to 16 percent of the total credit, with the instruction that small and marginal farmers should receive one and a half of the advances. This limit was subsequently raised to 40 percent of the total credit, with the instruction that 1 percent must be allocated for the extreme poor at an interest rate of 4 percent. The remainder of the sector would receive loans at an interest rate ranging from 10.5 to 14.5 percent, as opposed to the commercial rate of 19.5 percent. Furthermore, collateral requirements for these loans were reduced. In other words, the government asked banks to offer higher risk loans at a lower interest rate. This meant a greater proportion of the loan would not be recouped from the proceeds of the collateral should the borrowers default on their loans, and furthermore, no provision was made for non-performing loans. In short, the implementation of this programme would make the banking sector fragile. Although these measures increased the share of the 'priority sectors' in the credit market from 24.2 percent to 37.1 percent between 1976 and 1984, doubts remain about their effectiveness, particularly in relation to their improving small and marginal borrowers' access to the loan market.

For example, 57 percent of the total credit that was allocated to small enterprises was received by those whose net assets were over Rs 1million and who constituted 5 percent of the small enterprise population; those with assets ranging from Rs 100,000 to 1 million constituted 29 percent of the population and received 38 percent. This meant 95 percent of the allocated credit went to those whose net assets were over Rs 100,000. The remaining 5 percent of all the banks' allocated credit was received by those whose net assets fell below Rs 100,000 and accounted for 66 percent of the small enterprise population (RBI, 1979, Vol. 2, Tables 1–2).

In the 1970s anyone having net assets over Rs 100,000 would not be categorized as poor, but rather would be considered as having a fairly well-off enterprise. Furthermore, anyone having assets over Rs 1million would be considered as having a wealthy small enterprise. Lower socio-economic groups would fall within the range of those with net assets of less than Rs 1000 to Rs 100,000, and it is reasonable to suggest that those with a net investment of less than Rs 20,000 could be considered as poor. It is also reasonable to suggest that it is this group of enterprises that would have problems in meeting banks' collateral requirements. We do not know what proportion of the 5 percent of the bank credit that was received by enterprises with net assets of up to Rs 100,000, went to those who were below the Rs 20,000 benchmark. But in either case it is reasonable to suggest that the reduction in the collateral requirements did not improve these groups of borrowers' access to the loan market in any significant manner.[13]

A similar situation has also been observed in the case of rural households, i.e. rich landlords and middle-class farmers were able to take advantage of a much higher proportion of these cheap loanable funds than were their poorer counterparts (Basu, 1982). In fact, despite the reduction in the collateral requirements, access to the loan market was still systematically in favour of those who had larger assets; that is, the higher the value of the collateral, the greater the access to the loan market (RBI, 1987a, b).

This leads to an interesting question, which is why, despite the reductions in the collateral requirements and interest rates, do lenders still prefer to offer loans to relatively large borrowers? It is to this problem we turn now.

6.3   AN ANALYSIS OF INTERVENTION

The small firms' lesser access to the loan market mainly stems from their smaller scale of operation and lower asset value. This smaller scale of operation causes a greater constraint in reducing their unit cost of production as opposed to any large or medium sized firm. In addition to this, they have no control over the market price, which is largely influenced by large firms or wholesale traders. As a result their profit margin per unit of investment in general is lower than that of their larger counterparts. Even if they enjoy a higher profit margin in a particular sector due to a very high demand for the goods and services that sector provides, this does not suggest that they will be able to continue to enjoy such profit margins in the foreseeable future. This is due to easy entry conditions. This suggests that smaller firms are more vulnerable to the competitive atmosphere in which they operate, and to possible fluctuations in the aggregate demand, than larger counterparts. This vulnerability is further aggravated by the fact that they have either very few or no alternative means of subsidizing their business should it face any temporary adversaries. Furthermore, due to their smaller scale of operation, they require smaller loans, which in turn increases lenders' administrative costs. Thus given the interest rate, these loans offer a lower return, combined with greater uncertainty, which in turn reduces their expected profitability. As a result there is a lower demand for these clients in the lenders' market. In fact, banks in most cases remain the only avenue for small firms to raise capital from the formal loan market. In other words, banks enjoy near monopoly power when dealing with small firms as borrowers. This in turn reduces banks' necessity to take any credit risk. Furthermore, due to the presence of a ceiling on the interest rate (which used to exist in the early days), banks did not have any incentive to take credit risk on these loans. Thus when banks offer loans to small firms, they advance them by securing the entire loan by the credit standard. It is this which causes the small firms' inaccessibility to this loan market, as they are either unable or unwilling to meet such high credit standards. This problem is further complicated by the fact that, especially in the case of developing countries, the tangible assets that most small firms can offer as collateral are not recognized by banks. New firms or a start-up firm often have to meet an even higher credit standard than established small firms. This is mainly because they have no previous track record, and some businesses are started because of an inability to become part of the payroll of another business. In these situations it is reasonable for bankers to secure not only the principal but also the interest payment by collateral. This makes it almost impossible for a new firm to start a business with bank capital and as a result we observe that almost 80 to 90 percent of the new small firms' start-up finance mainly comes from their own savings or else from friends and relatives.[14] This is not only the case in developing countries but a similar situation has also been observed in developed countries as well, such as in the UK, USA and Australia (Basu, 1989).

Accordingly, governments in developed countries adopted certain policies to improve small businesses' access to the loan market, mostly comprising various loan guarantee schemes, ceilings on the interest rate, and so on, the majority of which largely remained ineffective. In the case of India, similar policies were adopted in the 1960s and they remained ineffective. However, in the 1970s the Indian government decided to strengthen these programmes by simultaneously introducing a quota system and reducing the collateral requirements. A quota system forces banks to offer loans to those they would otherwise refuse. A reduction in the collateral requirements removes any possible excuse that banks can present as to why they were unable to meet the quota requirement. By the early 1980s, banks were able to meet the government quota of 40 percent. Therefore it is reasonable to assume that banks would become fragile, because of the reduction in the collateral requirements. But what is not clear is why banks were still unable to make any significant inroads into the lower socio-economic groups' loan market.

In India, a small firm in 1970 was defined as one employing from 1 to 50 employees, with total net assets up to Rs 1.5 million (i.e. US$150,000), and this was raised to Rs 2.5 million in 1980. This meant small businesses ranged from extremely poor to wealthy, but the bulk of them were poor. In terms of access to the banks' loan market, it is reasonable to assume that those belonging to the middle to upper income bracket within the orbit of the priority sector would have some established connection with banks. This leaves the poor, the majority of whom fall outside the banks' loan market. They mostly received loans from the informal loan market. Detailed operational characteristics of this market are to some extent foreign to bank officers, and so too the characteristics of these borrowers, including their ability, are unknown to the bankers. Fragmented information that is available suggests that lenders demand collateral whose value exceeds the size of the loans and who set the interest rate at such a high level that it expropriates all the surplus that borrowers generate. Often lenders deliberately set the interest rate to such a high level that it forces borrowers to default on their loans, and the lender then expropriates the last bit of the asset that the borrower has mortgaged to the lender in order to obtain the loan.[15] Thus it is reasonable to assume that the Indian government adopted the policy of reducing the collateral requirements and offering loans at a lower interest rate, mainly to bring these poor borrowers within the orbit of the banks' loan market. The complexity of the problem arises here as a significant portion of this loan market falls outside the range of the fragmented information on which the policy was formulated.

Most of the investment in fixed capital by small businesses, whether they belong to the manufacturing or servicing sector, is small, and this is especially the case for small businesses whose size of operation could be described as tiny, and who mainly require loans for working capital. The majority do not own any land or buildings, operate in rented space and, in the case of manufacturing, some of them even rent machinery.

Therefore they do not have any recognized tangible assets to offer, against which they can seek loans. As a result most of the professional lenders abstain from entering into this loan market. Consequently, small businesses mainly rely on their own savings or else on friends and relatives. Those who seek loans from other than friends and relatives, if a manufacturer, mainly receive credit from traders, while those with retail shops either receive credit from wholesale traders or producers. This credit mainly comes in the form of inputs to manufacturers and in the form of goods to retail shops. Therefore this is mainly trade credit. Traders advance a loan to a small manufacturer in order to ensure the procurement of future output at a predetermined price, and repayment of the loan takes place at the time the trader collects the output, where it is deducted from the payment to the manufacturer. In the case of a retail shop, the loan takes place in the form of advancing goods on credit, and repayment occurs before the advance of the next lot of goods. In other words, the advance of the next amount of credit in the form of goods, is contingent on the borrower's repayment of the past debt.

It is important to recognize the difference in the operational characteristics between this loan market as opposed to the normal loan market. The normal loan market operates on the principle of interest rate, where the interest is the price of the loan, which induces lenders to advance loans, and unless the borrower can ensure the payment of this price, the lender cannot advance a loan. As there exists a time difference between the advance of a loan and its repayment, the borrower's tangible assets are mortgaged in the form of collateral, in order to ensure the payment of the price, including the principal, at some future date. As opposed to that, this loan market operates on the principle of procuring the future output in the case of a trader, where the trader advances inputs in the form of credit to a manufacturer. In the case of a retail shop it operates on the principle of being an additional outlet for the goods of wholesale traders and producers. Thus the lenders' inducement to offer loans to these borrowers principally arises from the procurement of the future output and an additional outlet for lenders to sell his/her goods and services.[16] The interest rate is not the main principle on which this market operates, and often a lender advances loans without stipulating the interest rate.[17]

Now let us take the case of traders and their reason for advancing loans to small manufacturers. They purchase goods from the manufacturer, sell them to another market and make a profit from the difference in the price between the two. The trader supplies goods to the market according to the amount ordered by his buyers. It is according to the order which a trader places that each manufacturer undertakes production. If one or two manufacturers cannot produce the quantity that the trader wants due to shortages in input or a lack of working capital, this means the trader will not be able to meet his commitment to the buyers. The trader cannot readily meet this shortfall by purchasing from another trader or from other manufacturers, since all of them operate on the basis of the orders that they have received from the market. Therefore, it is unlikely that there will be some surplus readily available to the trader. But the trader knows that for his future business it is important to meet the current commitment, which in turn establishes his reputation as a reliable supplier of goods. Thus once the trader establishes a connection with a certain number of manufacturers they become an important partner. Therefore each trader has an interest to ensure that his small manufacturers' output is not adversely affected by shortages in the input requirements, which principally arise from shortages in the small enterprises' working capital requirements. Thus they advance loans to these manufacturers, who, when they need a loan, mortgage their future output. For small manufacturers, these traders reduce the uncertainty that arises from the lack of knowledge in relation to the future demand for their product. Therefore the uncertainty faced by these small enterprises is reduced, not only in relation to how much to produce, but also in relation to where to sell it. Thus traders are very important outlets for these manufacturers' products. In other words, there exists an interdependent relationship between the traders and the small manufacturers, and as a result this loan market operates without collateral requirements.

Banks can only enter this market if this alternative loan system is non-existent,[18] if the interest rate is too high, or if the price that a trader offers to the manufacturers is so low that it does not allow them to retain any surplus. If the interest rate is too high, or the price that a particular trader offers is too low, then a rival trader will take over. This therefore suggests that neither the interest rate nor the price can go to these extremes, either of which is required to open the possibility for banks to enter into this market. Of course there are manufacturers who directly supply goods to the market and therefore do not use traders. But they are relatively prosperous, already have a connection with the banks so they can take a direct order from the market, and have achieved the economies of scale to carry out such activity without the assistance of traders. The problem for banks in entering the market where traders are already operating, is that firstly they have to ignore the issue of collateral completely, and secondly they have to provide information to these manufacturers about where to offload their products. The first will make the return of the banks' loan capital uncertain, while failure to provide the second will increase the uncertainty for the manufacturers as regards not only how much to produce but also where to sell it. Neither of these is possible for banks, and without them borrowers will not accept the condition of loans. This leaves the other option of the trader standing as a guarantor for these manufacturers, which a trader will not do without some personal gain.

This therefore may explain why, despite the reduction in the collateral requirements, banks in general are unable to enter into this market. Thus the reduction in the collateral requirements and the reduced interest rate mainly help those who could at best be described as the Keynesian 'fringe of borrowers', who do not have the first claim on the banks' loans. These are the borrowers who in the absence of government policy either receive loans of less than that demanded, or are often denied loans altogether at a higher interest rate. Now the reduced collateral requirements and interest rate mean these borrowers receive loans which exceed the value of the collateral they offer. This means the loan market will then attract a large number of bad borrowers.[19]

A similar situation has also been observed in the case of the rural sector. Traditionally commercial banks, at least in the case of India, have shown their reluctance to advance credit to the rural sector. This is because, in the case of agriculture, the return from its current investment is subject to the whims of nature, which always remain uncertain. This uncertainty in relation to future income in the case of the rural sector principally arises from four factors, two of which concern the rainfall: its level and its distribution. Thus the cultivable area, which is not under the control of an irrigational facility, is more susceptible to crop failure if the rainfall is below normal. Even normal rainfall may have an adverse consequence on the crop if its distribution affects the timing of the availability of water. These factors not only cause a variation in the yield per unit of land, but also cause a variation in the labour input requirements. For example, if the crop production is below normal, especially due to the poor distribution of rainfall, then less labour will be required during the harvest, but this could not be predicted during the sowing period, implying that part of the labour force will remain idle. Similarly, if the crop production is above normal, part of it may be lost in the absence of a reserve stock of labour to draw on at critical times. Also heavy rainfall may cause an outbreak of fever during the sowing period. Thirdly, an adverse financial situation may affect the health of the labour force during the harvest. Finally, the expectation of changes in the relative price ratios of competing crops introduces uncertainty in relation to the allocation of resources among different crops for individual farmers. All of these factors amount to uncertainty in relation to future rates of return on an investment in the agricultural sector.[20] In addition to this, the majority of farmers are poor and do not have any alternative assets to rely on to meet bank payments should the crop production fall below its expected level. Furthermore, the administrative cost of advancing these loans is high due to their smaller size, raising doubts about their profitability even if no default takes place. As a result, despite government insistence in the 1950s and 1960s, apart from government-sponsored cooperatives and land mortgage banks, commercial banks remained reluctant to participate in providing credit facilities to this sector as well. The private lenders who operate here are those who directly derive their living from agriculture, e.g. landlords, grain traders and local shopkeepers. The loan market that was developed here also originated from a congruence of interest, similar to that described above.

However, by the late 1960s it became quite clear that unless and until substantial capital could be injected into the rural sector, the growing inequality between urban and rural areas could not be reduced. As stated earlier in this chapter, by the mid 1960s the government adopted the High Yielding Variety Programme (HYVP) in order to achieve self-sufficiency in food production. HYV seed offers a higher yield per unit of land compared with the local variety of seeds, and furthermore its shorter maturity period opens up scope for double to multiple cropping. Thus the programme offered a solution for the food problem, and provided the opportunity for double to multiple cropping, which in turn opened up the possibility of increasing the number of days of employment for farmers. On paper, it therefore offered an avenue to directly attack the issue of poverty by not only increasing the number of days of employment, but also by increasing farmers' income, and indirectly through the reduction in the price of food via its higher availability. However, this programme was much more costly than cultivation with the local variety, because HYV seeds require much higher doses of chemical fertilizers and an assured water supply. This further increased the government's urgency to inject a substantial amount of capital into agriculture. Accordingly, the government declared that a little over half of the credit facilities that were allocated to the priority sector must go to agriculture.

In order to promote HYV cultivation the government also declared that a loan preference would be given to those who adopted the HYVP. As HYV cultivation required an assured water supply, this meant loans must be allocated to farmers who either had controlled irrigational facilities, or had sufficient land to make the installation of irrigational facilities economically viable. Most irrigational facilities are either owned or controlled by rich landlords and middle class farmers. For those who did not have irrigational facilities, if they had a minimum of 10 acres of land then it was considered economically viable to install one. This meant the credit directed programme benefited those who adopted the HYVP, who happened to be rich and middle class farmers. In other words, of the 80 percent of farming households whose holding size fell below 10 acres, a majority would be denied the HYVP, unless they had the benefit of canal irrigation. Initially these farmers obtained loans for the installation of irrigational facilities and the purchase of inputs. Thus the initial allocation of loans was mostly invested in devices which could be categorized as land saving devices.

Consequently, the value of their land increased, compared with those whose land size was not sufficient to make the installation of irrigational facilities economically viable, and in the process it further increased their access to the loan market. Thus the government policy of reduced collateral requirements and a cheaper rate not only benefited these borrowers, but in the process it further enhanced their access to the loan market. This was largely because of the fact that as cheaper rates reduced the repayment rate on loans, borrowers could borrow larger amounts than would have been possible at a higher rate, and because of the reduced collateral requirements, they did not have to offer collateral of a higher value as is required under normal banking operations.

As a result these borrowers received more loans of a considerably larger size than was possible in the absence of this policy and subsequently they used these loans to purchase machinery which was mainly categorized as labour saving devices, e.g. tractors and threshing machines.[21] Thus this government policy, instead of increasing it, has reduced the scope of employment in the rural area. Also as the greater proportion of loans were concentrated in the hands of rich landlords and middle-class farmers, this further aggravated the unequal distribution of income and wealth in the rural sector. Thus in the case of agriculture, the aggravation of unequal distribution of income and wealth is largely attributable to the government policy. Needless to say, whatever attempts were made to reach the poorest farmers, it was found that their loan market also operates on the basis of a congruence of interest similar to that which we described above, and therefore could not make any appreciable inroads.[22]

Thus when one examines the performance of the priority sector with its specified poverty alleviation scheme, it is not unreasonable to claim that this programme benefited mostly the middle to wealthy class, both in the case of small enterprises and in the case of the rural sector. This may have contributed to the rise in the overall capital intensity, realized in the GDCF (Gross Domestic Capital Formation), which rose from 18.2 to 24.7 percent between 1965/66 and 1981/82. But their contribution to the overall GDP remained marginal, i.e. the rate of growth of output, which was 4.10 percent per year between 1950 and 1966, rose marginally to 4.14 percent between 1971/72 and 1981/82.[23] But in the process, the reduced collateral requirements exposed banks' capital to higher levels of credit risk. This problem was further heightened by the fact that the lower margins between the loan rate and deposit rate did not permit banks to adequately incorporate the expected cost of non-performing loans. But the government's action reduced this margin greatly, thereby making banks vulnerable to even a few defaults, implying that in the event of such defaults on loans, they would be making an operating loss. Thus the form of intervention implemented by Indian policy makers, no matter how noble their intention, became counter-productive.

6.4 CONCLUSION

The analysis presented in this chapter suggests that there was a need for intervention in order to mobilize higher levels of savings and to allocate credit to the more productive areas of the economy. However, by the 1960s it became increasingly clear that the commercial banks were not likely to participate willingly in all aspects of the government's development programme. Commercial banks in particular remained reluctant to offer loans to the small business and rural sectors. Banks' refusal principally arose because these loans offered a lower return and higher risk compared with any large loans. It became necessary for the government to rethink its strategy in relation to how to increase the return and reduce the risk on loans, especially small loans. One way to achieve these two goals is to offer group loans. Group loans reduce the administrative costs that are involved in each small unit of loan, thereby increasing the return per unit, and in addition, by holding the group responsible for the performance of the loan, reduce its riskiness. This is because with this arrangement, if any individual member of the group defaults, then the entire group will be denied a loan in the future.

Instead, the Indian government did just the opposite, i.e. it decided to reduce the collateral requirements and interest rate, thereby increasing the credit risk and reducing the return on these loans. Furthermore, by taking this course of action the government overlooked an important problem that is likely to emerge, and which is normally taken care of by the credit standard requirements, i.e. the possibility of the emergence of moral hazard.

This problem particularly arises in the case of long-term loans for the purchase of fixed capital (e.g. a minibus), where the borrower may consider it a one-off loan. Furthermore, in the presence of weak bankruptcy laws these borrowers also know that they can get away without paying any penalty for their default on loans. They are unlikely to be concerned about their credit rating. Thus by reducing the collateral requirements, the Indian government not only exposed the banks' loan capital to higher levels of credit risk but also introduced the possibility of inviting many bad borrowers.

The Indian government undertook this policy mainly to provide cheaper credit facilities to poor borrowers, but observation reveals that poor borrowers did not receive much benefit. This is because the policy that was adopted by the Indian government was aimed at replacing the loan market which was under the control of private moneylenders. But the bulk of the poor do not have access to the private moneylenders' market, because they have either insufficient assets or no tangible assets to offer as collateral against which they can seek a loan. In fact, our analysis suggests that a sizeable portion of the poor borrowers' loan market was under the control of traders, landlords and producers. In the absence of any loan facility for these borrowers, this loan market was born out of an endogenous process to meet the needs of both parties and operated on the basis of personal relationships, in the case of both small enterprises and the agricultural sector. In other words, this market operates on the basis of a congruence of interest. Therefore its operational characteristics are very different from those of the normal loan market and it operates without the normal collateral requirements. Thus the policy of reduced collateral requirements could not replace the non-collateral requirements. This problem was further exacerbated by the fact that this market had some additional requirements, for example, in the case of a small manufacturer where there was a need to provide marketing facilities, banks could not provide these facilities, and as a result could not penetrate this market. Consequently, the policy of reduced collateral requirements, lower interest rates and the implementation of the quota system mainly benefited wealthy small businesses as well as the wealthy farming community. These are the borrowers who either already had an established connection with the banks or could have established such a connection without the aid of this policy. However with the help of this policy they received the bulk of the loans by meeting the lower credit standards. Thus when they defaulted on loans, banks were left with little option other than to carry the cost of non-performing loans. Therefore this policy aggravated the unequal distribution of income and wealth, especially in the rural areas, and increased the fragility of the banks as a whole, without improving poor borrowers' access to the formal loan market in any appreciable manner.[24]

NOTES

1. Although South Korea initially adopted an import substitution policy, after a brief period it decided to switch to an export-led growth policy when it recognized possible outlets for its products, especially in Japan. Japan abandoned the production of high wage items due to rises in the real wage, and South Korea, being a former colony of Japan, recognized that it could capture this market.

2. Although from the mid-1960s onwards, India recognized the difficulty in industrializing the nation by following the import substitution policy, it could not opt out. India devalued its currency, but exports did not increase as anticipated. This was because of low supply elasticities. Sectors which had shown some rise in exports, such as engineering, mainly owed this to an increase in excess capacity in the capital goods sector, as a result of a slackening in public investment. Furthermore, it could not totally liberalize its imports owing to foreign currency constraints. In this situation liberalization meant India had to accumulate massive foreign debt, which could only be repaid from export surpluses. This meant a massive rise in its export earnings was required prior to the liberalization of imports. But policy makers could not foresee this possibility in the presence of the high protection that Indian goods faced in the rich countries' markets, especially in the textile market. As a result, it could not see any immediate gain in switching from import substitution to export-led growth. See Chakravarty (1987b) for further details on this issue. Furthermore, it is important to recognize that despite South Korea's high growth rate in exports, by 1970 it could not retire its foreign debt, and in fact it was increasing, largely as a consequence of the high import component in their export items. As a result South Korea too decided to develop its heavy engineering sector, and impose a heavy restriction on these items until it improved its international competitiveness (see Westphal, 1990). Apart from that, the Indian government never had the kind of authority required to develop successful export industries. For this kind of analysis see Fields (1984). The basic argument here is that relative wage differentials do not tell us the entire story, but a certain amount of authoritarian power is required to

ensure the maintenance of quality and the timeliness of meeting the target (see also Chakravarty, 1987b). See Ahluwalia (1998) for the difficulties that the Indian government has faced in recent years in implementing reforms that were necessary for the infrastructural development.

3. This problem was further exacerbated by the fact that India relied more on its own domestic savings for development, as opposed to foreign savings as in the case of South Korea.

4. It is important to note that the Indian government's intervention did not always necessarily follow from an analysis of market failure, but arose from the fact that the policy makers had little confidence in the market to deliver the goods, which belief could have been accentuated by historical events. As a result intervention itself became a part of life. For details see Dasgupta (1993).

5. For example, in 1956 SBI and its associates were directed to open 400 branch facilities in the rural and semi-urban areas in the next five years (RBI, 1969).

6. The rising operating cost might have been further accentuated by the fact that in 1972, in order to reduce the unemployment rate of new graduates, the government put pressure on the public sector banks to directly recruit some of them. This caused overmanning in the public sector banks. In fact, this recruitment caused the number of staff to exceed the number of available desks in certain branches, and managers often had to develop roster systems for these young graduates. Under this roster system the graduates were not required to attend the office every day, but as they were employed as full-time employees they received a monthly salary.

7. For a detailed account of each of the respective organizations' principal functions and structures and for details of various other institutions see Sen and Vaidya (1997).

8. The IDBI provided 90 percent of the cost of the fixed capital expenditure as loans by mortgaging land and plant and equipment, while banks provided 75 percent of the working capital requirements by mortgaging raw materials, work in progress and finished goods.

9. These wholesale traders, often referred to as hoarders in India, used to purchase the above mentioned items just after the harvest and then sell them before the next harvesting season began, when their prices used to soar due to their scarcity. They used to make a windfall profit from the price difference between the two seasons. This form of hoarding had an adverse impact on inflation and was considered a socially undesirable act. Therefore the offering of loans by banks to these borrowers was not greatly appreciated by many. But from the banks' point of view; (a) these loans were essentially short-term, and therefore did not have an adverse impact upon their liquidity position; and (b) the return from these loans was almost certain. This is because as long as insufficiency remains in the production of necessary items, price differences will emerge between the two seasons and the hoarder will make a windfall profit. This in turn eliminates the possibility of default on these loans. Thus the combination of (a) and (b) increases banks' profitability at a very high rate and therefore these borrowers are considered as very valuable customers to the banks. This brought a serious conflict between the private banks and the government, which principally arose from the irreconcilable dispute that often emerges between private profitability and social desirability. A similar issue can also be raised when banks offer loans for stock market or foreign currency speculation purposes.

10. These schemes are similar to licensing scheme arrangements, which introduce the possibility for corruption to emerge. See Bhagwati and Desai (1970) for further details.

11. Even in 1970, a year and a half after the banks were nationalized, 83.4 percent of the total commercial bank advances still went to industry and commerce and their principal clients remained large borrowers, with agriculture receiving only 4.3 percent of the total advances (Krishnaswamy *et al.*, 1987).

12. In June 1969, the government nationalized 14 of its largest banks, each of which had deposits of Rs 500 million or more. When taking into account the SBI and its associated banks, 22 of the largest banks accounted for 86 percent of total deposits, and these all came under the control of the government. In 1980 six more banks were nationalized (Krishnaswamy *et al.*, 1987).

13. This distribution had not changed even by the early 1980s, as the only change was in the definition of a small business, i.e. instead of being a firm with net assets of up to Rs 1 to 1.5 million, this was raised so a firm with net assets of up to Rs 2 to 2.5 million or employing more than 50 workers was considered a small business. With this change in the definition, by the early 1980s small enterprises received 13 percent of the total bank advances, about half of which went to those small enterprises whose undepreciated value of plant and equipment ranged between Rs 2 million to 2.5 million, and which employed more than 50 employees. These would be considered as medium-sized firms in other developing countries (Little *et al.*, 1989).

14. For an excellent survey of this issue see Little *et al.* (1987), where these authors point out the principal barriers to small businesses obtaining loans is their inability to meet lenders' collateral requirements, a reason for which even private moneylenders abstain from offering loans to these small enterprises.

15. See Bhaduri (1977) on this issue.

16. For example, in the case of powerlooms, industry traders are the principal suppliers of credit (Little *et al.*, 1987). Similarly, in the case of small retail shops; for example, a small cigarette shop in Calcutta situated in a fairly centrally located area not only receives cigarettes, but also soft drinks such as coke, on trade credit. The small retail shops that are situated in a small town such as Bolpur (which is 100 miles from Calcutta), also often receive trade credit indirectly from the wholesale traders. In this situation, wholesale traders will advance goods to traders whom we refer to as daily passengers. They are called this because they travel to Calcutta every day by train after collecting orders from the local small shop keepers and place orders accordingly with the wholesale traders, where they receive the goods on credit. Then they return to the town by the midnight train and deliver the goods to the local shops and receive their payment plus commission, either immediately or later, depending on the arrangements made with each shop. But their next lot of goods on credit depends on the wholesale traders being paid for the previous lot. All these daily passengers come from lower socio-economic groups. The entire chain of this operation works on the basis of a congruence of interest.

17. For example, it was revealed that in a survey of Bombay city 95.7 percent of the loans that were advanced by the traders were at zero interest rate (Karkal, 1967).

18. The Bangladesh Grameen Bank is a prime example, which opened a loan market for the landless females in Bangladesh, a market which was non-existent before. This bank, which specializes in group lending, recognizes that these landless women do not have any tangible assets, either as a group or individually, to offer as collateral against which they can seek a loan. To replace the collateral requirements, while not exposing banks' capital to a higher level of credit risk, each member from the group (which is composed of a self-selected group of five people from the same village) is asked to make a small weekly contribution to their savings deposits. Several weeks after the group is formed, two members from the group receive the loan. A 5 percent fee is charged on all loans at initiation, and this fund, combined with the group's total savings, is then used as a security against the loans which are advanced. This security is divided into two parts, one comprising an emergency consumption fund, covering funeral and wedding obligations and the second to protect against the default on loans. Given this arrangement, if the initial two borrowers make their weekly payments then two other members receive loans, and so on. In addition to these arrangements, a further rule was introduced that if any member of the group

defaults, then the entire group becomes ineligible for future access to the Bangladesh Grameen Bank. In general, defaults mainly arise when one or two members from the group become sick and as a result their earnings decline, in which case it becomes important for the other members to subsidize their sick members. There are two possible sources of default among the poor, apart from crop failure. One arises from unexpected consumption needs and the other from temporary illness among members of the group. The Grameen Bank addresses both of these issues by making provision for emergency consumption loans, and by holding the entire group responsible for any individual member's default which in turn reduces the possibility of default. In addition, group savings plus the fees on loans provide the security against which the loans are advanced. For further details see Khandker *et al.* (1995) and World Bank (1989).

19. In fact, in the case of transport operations, loans were advanced for the purchase of rickshaws, scooter rickshaws and minibuses. These loans ranged from Rs 600 to Rs 90,000 (at 1970s prices) and no equity was required on these loans. The recipients of these loans mainly came from lower socio-economic groups, but they were associated with the political parties who were then in government. None of these loans was honoured.

20. See Dasgupta (1970) for further details on this issue.

21. It appears that the above result might have been accentuated by the fact that long-term loans with a lower interest rate reduce the cost of capital to such an extent that, despite the presence of a very low wage rate, landlords recognized a possible gain can be made by reducing their reliance on labour. This gain does not necessarily follow from the urge to reduce the wage bill, but appears to follow from the fact that where there is backward technology, manpower is the most precious asset which one can buy, which means that in conjunction with wages, landlords have to offer other benefits in order to ensure a steady availability (or flow) of labour, when necessary. These benefits are not only non-accountable in wage bills, but some of them are not even accountable in monetary units, as it involves time and effort to develop and manage a relationship between the landlords and labourers which ensures a steady flow of labour, which at times could be conceived as quite costly (see Basu, 1997 for details). Consequently, landlords could not forgo the opportunity to opt for labour saving devices, but unfortunately these devices are not necessarily accompanied by an improvement in land productivity.

22. See Basu (1997) for further details on this issue.

23. See Krishnaswamy *et al.* (1987) for further details.

24. As the past policies failed to live up to their promises, India, too, liberalized its financial markets. For details of this process see Sen and Vaidya (1997). Although this process started in the 1980s for some reason 1991 was marked as the year of liberalization. Throughout the 1980s and 1990s stock market activity continued to rise without adding to growth in the real economy. In fact, it is interesting to note that during the years when the stock market did not do well, i.e. between 1995 and 1997, the real economy expanded at a rate of nearly 7 percent per annum (Singh, 1998). Since then the Indian economy has slowed down, despite the optimism shown by the reformers. In fact, following liberalization in India in 1991 there was a sharp rise in rural poverty and subsequently the government had to intervene (Tendulkar, 1998). From then onwards the process of reform has slowed. See Bhagwati (1998b) and Srinivasan (1998 and 2000) for more on this issue. Therefore it is too early to assess the full impact of these reforms.

7. Concluding remarks

The analysis that has been presented in this book suggests that the loan market operates in the presence of uncertainty and as a result the interest rate alone does not clear it.

In this market, the lender will ask for collateral or some form of security, which is referred to as the credit standard, to ensure that should the borrower's project fail, the borrower has an alternative means to honour his/her debt obligation. Therefore any borrower who is unable to meet a bank's credit standard requirements will either be denied the loan or will receive less than that demanded.

But the puzzling problem is that the banks do not maintain a uniform credit standard for all borrowers. This in turn causes a variation in the borrowers' access to the loan market. This variation principally arises as the credit standard enters into the loan equation, which suggests that those who will be able to offer collateral of greater value will be able to obtain a larger loan. As the per unit administrative cost for larger loans falls below that for smaller loans with a given interest rate, larger loans will offer higher expected rates of return compared with their smaller counterparts.

Large loans are normally demanded by large firms. Large firms, due to their larger size of operation, in general are more likely to enjoy economies of scale of production compared with their smaller counterparts. This means they are more likely to enjoy lower costs per unit of production, given the market price of the product. Furthermore, due to their larger size of operation they do have some control over the price of their product as opposed to their smaller counterparts. This therefore suggests that large firms will be in a better position to absorb any adverse shocks that may follow from fluctuations in the state of the economy than will their smaller counterparts. In addition to this, they have assets of greater value, which suggests that should the return from the projects (for which they seek loans) fall below the expected return, they have more than sufficient alternative means to maintain their contractual payment. The combined impact of the lower administrative cost with a lesser likelihood of default increases the expected rate of return on larger loans at a much higher level than that of any smaller loans.

The above analysis therefore suggests that in the lenders' market, there will be a high demand for borrowers who offer a higher expected rate of return on loans compared with other borrowers. This higher demand in turn will increase the competition among lenders to attract borrowers who demand larger loans. To attract these borrowers lenders therefore will offer certain concessions, one of which includes a reduction in the credit standard requirements. In other words, lenders will be prepared to take a greater credit risk on these loans. This means as the borrowers' ability to offer higher expected rates of return falls, so too does the demand for these borrowers in the lenders' market, and therefore lenders will not take credit risk on loans which offer lower expected rates of return.

Thus it is the variation in the credit standard requirements for different borrowers which explains why access to the loan market differs between two individuals. But this variation is driven by the difference in the expected rates of return from the two loans. Thus the variation in access to the loan market for different groups of borrowers principally arises from the difference in the expected rates of return on loans that these different groups offer.

As the uncertainty factor was replaced by certainty equivalence, the importance of the credit standard in the lender's decision to advance a loan was overlooked. This left policy makers with the impression that it is the imperfection in the loan market arising from lenders' oligopolistic or monopolistic power that allows them to practise a discriminatory lending policy. This in turn causes a variation in the borrowers' access to the loan market. Accordingly, past policies focused on how to neutralize or to eliminate the adverse impact of the imperfectly competitive market. But what was not recognized was that the logic of the operation of the market that follows from the uncertainty principle, will bear little or no resemblance to the logic of the operation of the market that follows from the assumption of certainty equivalence.

When the past policy failed to live up to its expectations, or to put it more precisely, when it failed to bring allocative efficiency, the proponents of the school of liberalization put forward their view that it is government intervention which causes a distortion in the operation of the loan market. They argued that the mandatory ceiling on interest rates and the numerous lending restrictions that were imposed on banks were the principal reasons for the variation in access to the loan market between different groups of borrowers. Furthermore, they argued that the existence of the lenders' monopolistic or oligopolistic power over the borrowers, arising from the government imposed barriers to entry, allowed these lenders to practise a discriminatory lending policy. According to them, the ceiling on interest rates does not permit banks to incorporate the additional risk, over and above the normal risk that is involved in some loans, into the calculation of the interest rate, and as a result banks deny loans to high risk borrowers. Furthermore, the existence of the monopolistic or oligopolistic power of the lenders over borrowers reduces their urge to offer loans to those who offer higher risk, and as a result they offer loans only to those who offer lower risk. The assumption here is that the risk and return represent a positive linear relationship. Accordingly they argued that the ceiling on interest rates and the varieties of restrictions that were imposed on the banks became counter-productive. In other words, these forms of intervention not only allowed bankers to continue the practice of a discriminatory lending policy, but also in the process produced a lower growth rate than otherwise one would have experienced. Accordingly, they recommended the policy of liberalization, which meant the removal of all forms of restrictions that were imposed on the banks in the past. This in turn would allow banks to offer risk-adjusted interest rates, and therefore banks would have an incentive to offer loans to those who offer higher risk. Also, the injection of greater competition by increasing the number of lenders in the market would encourage banks to engage in more risky, high yielding investments, provided negative shock would not make these investments less profitable. Thus the overall implication of this policy thrust was that the loan capital would tend to move from less risky, low yielding investments to more risky, high yielding investments, and therefore would bring efficiency in investment, which in turn would produce a higher growth rate.

The risk referred to here is that risk which arises from the nature of the project, and thus risk differentials refer to project risk differentials. But no attention was given to the risk differentials arising from the difference in the size of operation and the asset backing between two borrowers, a consideration of which might have suggested that the risk and return may not be represented by a positive linear relationship.

However, without risking a repetition of the argument that has already been presented, we will confine ourselves to some general remarks. To begin with, in the absence of recognition of the issue of uncertainty, it appears that this analysis followed from the assumption that the issue of security principally arises from the lack of facility to offer risk-adjusted interest rates. In other words, the assumption was that security is the substitute for the lack of facility to offer risk-adjusted interest rates. But no recognition was given to the fact that it was the lenders' inability to calculate the precise magnitude of the risk that led to the security element or the credit standard entering into the loan contract. Consequently it was not recognized that the variation in access to the loan market for different groups of borrowers arose not so much from the lack of facility to offer risk-adjusted interest rates, but from the difference in the expected rates of return between loans. As stated above, this difference in the expected rate of profitability between different loans principally arises from the different values of the assets that different borrowing groups offer and against which they demand a different size of loan. Therefore the variation in access to the loan market which mainly arises from borrowers offering higher or lower expected rates of return on loans, is unlikely to be removed either by making a provision to offer risk-adjusted interest rates or by injecting a higher level of competition into the lenders' market. Instead an increment in competition is more likely to be concentrated at that end of the market where borrowers offer higher expected rates of return, thereby leaving little spillover effect for the remaining competition to be felt in the smaller borrowers' loan market.

Interest rates surged shortly after liberalization and the competition among the lending institutions also surged for a brief period. But neither the higher interest rates nor this competition improved the small and marginal borrowers' access to the loan market. Instead competition concentrated at that end of the market where the borrowers offered higher expected rates of return on loans, and as a result it further forced banks to reduce their credit standard requirements which in turn increased the credit risk on these loans. But it neither increased investment in fixed capital nor led to a switch from low return to high return projects; instead investors made their switch from fixed capital investments to the acquisition of financial assets. As this switch was largely followed by expected changes in the price of financial assets, in the process loan returns also became locked in with the return that followed from this change. Thus it was only a matter of time before the actual price fell short of the expected price, and these borrowers had difficulty in maintaining their repayment rate. The banks were highly exposed to credit risk and this suggests that the alternative assets of these borrowers that were in the possession of the banks may not have been sufficient to meet the shortfall in this repayment rate. In this situation a banking crisis was inevitable. Thus as it stands today, financial liberalization, despite its claims, has neither been able to improve borrowers' access to the loan market nor to deliver a higher growth rate, and instead has been followed by a trail of financial distress.

Thus the fundamental problem with this policy was that its proponents appeared to make little attempt to understand the complications in which this market operates.

The experience of liberalization suggests that, whatever our philosophical view may be in relation to how the market should operate, government intervention will be required. This will be necessary both to prevent financial crisis, and to achieve a higher growth rate and to improve those borrowers' access to the loan market who otherwise will be denied loans. But the intervention adopted in the past also adversely affected the performance of the financial sector without necessarily always fulfilling its objectives, as we have observed in the cases of India and South Korea. It appears that financial liberalization may have followed from this failure.

Our investigation in the context of developing countries suggests that while the policy makers placed a greater emphasis on the mobilization of savings and the allocation of cheaper credit facilities to their preferred sectors, they paid little attention to the uncertainty factor. This was true for both South Korea and India.

In the case of South Korea, the government largely concentrated on organizing large loans for the development of certain sectors, where their principal clients were large firms. In order to provide cheaper credit to these firms, the government introduced discriminatory interest rates, that is, the cheapest credit was received by the preferred sectors. The interest rate was so low on these loans that the interest rate on deposits often exceeded it. In addition to this, the issue of the credit standard was ignored. Therefore for a period of 30 years South Korean banks carried a very high credit risk. In the early period of its development, whenever these firms were unable to maintain their loan repayment rates, the government bailed them out at the cost of the banks. Banks were allowed neither to make provision for the non-performing loans nor to address the issue of the credit standard, with the result that they remained fragile.

In the case of India, the government concentrated not only on organizing large loans for large projects, but also on allocating loans for the lower socio-economic groups. In the latter case it was an attempt to free these borrowers from the exploitative hands of the moneylenders. Thus the interest rates and the credit standard requirements on these loans were reduced, without the recognition that a large part of this market not only falls outside the operation of the private moneylenders' market but operates on the basis of a congruence of interest. Thus the programme by and large was unable to help the poor for whom the interest rates were reduced. Instead the reduced interest rates and credit standard requirements benefited mainly the large landowning class, middle-class farmers and wealthy small businesses (who in many other countries would be considered medium sized businesses).

In both of these countries, banks were used as instruments to allocate credit to their preferred sectors, and the issue of the profitability of the banks was never questioned. In other words, the fact that banks form an independent sector just like any other, and that this sector's survival too depends on profitability, was hardly given any consideration. Thus it is no wonder that this sector's fragility increased over time.

Therefore while the above analysis suggests that intervention will be required, it is necessary to ensure that the process of intervention does not increase the fragility of this sector. Experience suggests that the decision to reduce the banks' profitability by reducing the interest rate below the market rate in favour of increasing the social benefit, is a very short lived policy as it only transfers the profit from one sector to another. Therefore this brings conflict between the two sectors and in the process it increases the fragility of the banking sector, and therefore becomes counter-productive. Thus the policy should aim at achieving a balance, that is maximizing the social benefit, subject to constraint, without adversely affecting the banks' profitability. This is an area which falls outside the scope of this book but requires further work, and perhaps there are some lessons to be learned from the market which operates largely under the influence of a congruence of interest.

In the context of development, at least in the early stages, there is no doubt that some of the projects have to carry higher credit risk; otherwise those projects would not be undertaken. In this situation there is a need to develop very strong and enforceable bankruptcy laws, so that at least the moral hazard problem can be avoided. Secondly, there is a need to encourage firms to reduce debt/equity ratios in the foreseeable future, so that any shortfall in the loan repayment that may arise from a firm's loss of revenue due to demand deficiency, can be made up from the return on equity. Thirdly, it is necessary to encourage borrowing firms to develop an alternative pool of assets from part of their profits which then can be offered to banks as collateral, rather than purely concentrating on the growth of the firm. This in turn will unlock the fate of the banks' loan capital from the performance of the indebted firms. The third policy, to be fully effective, would take a considerable number of years to establish, during which period it would be necessary to give greater authority to banks to monitor these firms' performance. In some cases, it may be possible to encourage firms to merge or to join with other firms to raise the large loans that are required to finance major projects.

In the case of smaller and marginal borrowers, it may be necessary to offer group lending rather than individual loans, as has been introduced by the Bangladesh Grameen Bank. Group lending has a number of advantages. To begin with, the size of the group loans would be bigger than that of the small individual loans, and therefore would reduce the administrative cost per unit of loan, thereby increasing their expected rate of profitability. Secondly, if all members are held equally responsible for the performance of the loan, then the possibility of default that often arises from illness of individuals can be avoided, as the other members of the group will be obligated to subsidize the sick person. In certain instances it may be necessary to investigate the operational characteristics of the market, i.e. if the market operates on the basis of a congruence of interest, then it would be necessary to form cooperatives. We require further research in this area.

The analysis that has been presented here suggests that policies of the past as well as the present have not given adequate attention to the uncertainty aspect of the operation of this market, and as a result implementation of both policies adversely affected the performance of this sector. Therefore, it is important to recognize that this market operates in the presence of uncertainty and as a result, prior to formulating any policy, it is necessary to give adequate attention to developing precautionary measures, so that the policies neither lead to crisis nor increase this sector's fragility. In the past, attention has not been given to this issue. Experience suggests the cost of financial crisis is more heavily borne by the poorest of the poor, although often they may not be participants in this sector.

References

Agarwala, R.K. (1983), *Price Distortions and Growth in Developing Countries*, World Bank Staff Working Papers, No. 575, Washington, DC: The World Bank.

Ahluwalia, M.S. (1998), 'Infrastructure Development in India's Reforms,' in I.J. Ahluwalia and I.M.D. Little (eds) *India's Economic Reforms and Development Essays for Manmohan Singh*, Delhi: Oxford University Press.

Amsden, A.H. (1989), *Asia's Next Giant: South Korea and Late Industrialisation*, New York: Oxford University Press.

Amsden, A.H. (1994), 'Why Isn't the Whole World Experimenting with the East Asian Model to Develop?: Review of the East Asian Miracle', *World Development*, Vol. 22, pp. 627–33.

Amsden, A.H. and Euh Yoon-Dae (1993), 'South Korea's Financial Reforms: Good-Bye Financial Repression (Maybe), Hello New Institutional Restraints', *World Development*, Vol. 21, pp. 379–90.

Angell, J.W. (1960), 'Appropriate Monetary Policies and Operations in the United States Today', *Review of Economics and Statistics*, Vol. 42, pp. 247–52.

Arestis, P. and P. Demetriades (1996), 'Finance and Growth: Institutional Considerations and Causality', paper presented at the Royal Economic Society Annual Conference, Swansea University, April.

Arestis, P. and P. Demetriades (1997), 'Financial Development and Economic Growth: Assessing the Evidence', *Economic Journal*, Vol. 107, pp. 783–99.

Arestis, P. and M. Glickman (2002), 'Financial Crisis in South East Asia: Dispelling Illusion the Minskyan Way', *Cambridge Journal of Economics* (forthcoming).

Arndt, H. (1987), *Economic Development: The History of an Idea*, Chicago and London: Chicago University Press.

Arrow, K. (1962), 'The Economic Implications of Learning by Doing', *Review of Economic Studies*, Vol. 29, pp. 155–73.

Azzi, C.R. and J.C. Cox (1976), 'A Theory and Test of Credit Rationing: Comment', *American Economic Review*, Vol. 66, pp. 911–17.

Bagchi, A. K. (1992), 'Land Tax, Property Rights and Peasant Insecurity in Colonial India', *Journal of Peasant Studies*, Vol. 20, pp. 1–49.

Baltensperger, E. (1978), 'Credit Rationing: Issues and Questions', *Journal of Money, Credit and Banking*, Vol. 10, pp. 170–83.

Bank of Korea (1973), *Report on the Result of the August 3, 1972 Presidential Emergency Decree*, Seoul.

Bank of Korea (1985), *Annual Report*, Seoul.

Bank of Korea (1989), *Annual Report*, Seoul.

Bank of Korea (1994), *Annual Report*, Seoul.

Bank of Korea (1995), *Annual Report*, Seoul.

Bardhan, P.K. and A. Rudra (1978), 'Interlinkage of Land, Labour and Credit Relations: An Analysis of Village Survey Data in East India', *Economic and Political Weekly*, Vol. 13, Annual No., February.

Basu, K. (1983), 'The Emergence of Isolation and Interlinkage in Rural Markets', *Oxford Economic Papers*, Vol. 35, pp. 262–80.

Basu, K. (1984), *The Less Developed Economy: A Critique of Contemporary Theory*, Oxford: Basil Blackwell.

Basu, S. (1982), *An Analysis of the High Yielding Variety Programme in India*, MEc Dissertation, Sydney: Sydney University.

Basu, S. (1986), 'Problems of Small Business', *Economic Papers*, Vol. 5, pp. 92–110.

Basu, S. (1989), 'Deregulation: Small Business Access to the Capital Market – Theoretical Issues with Special Reference to Australian Bank Finance', *Australian Economic Papers*, Vol. 28, pp. 141–59.

Basu, S. (1992), *Asymmetric Information, Credit Rationing and the Stiglitz and Weiss Model*, Research Paper No. 360, School of Economic and Financial Studies, Sydney: Macquarie University.

Basu, S. (1994), 'Deregulation of the Australian Banking Sector: A Theoretical Perspective', *Australian Economic Papers*, Vol. 33, pp. 272–85.

Basu, S. (1996), 'The Theory of Credit Rationing Revisited', paper presented at the 1996 India and South East Asia Meeting of the Econometric Society, Delhi School of Economics, Delhi, December.

Basu, S. (1997), 'Why Institutional Credit Agencies are Reluctant to Lend to the Rural Poor: A Theoretical Analysis of the Indian Rural Credit Market', *World Development*, Vol. 25, pp. 267–80.

Basu, S. (1998), 'Why Do Banks Fail?, paper presented at the Economists Conference, organized by the Economic Society of Australia and New Zealand, held at the University of Sydney, Sydney.

Basu, S. (2001), 'Incomplete Information and Asymmetric Information', *Zagreb International Review of Economics and Business* (forthcoming).

Basu, S. (2002), 'Financial Fragility: Is It Rooted in the Development Process? An Examination with Special Reference to the South Korean Experience', *International Papers in Political Economy* (forthcoming).

Beckerman, P. (1997), 'Central Bank Decapitalization in Developing Economies', *World Development*, Vol. 25, pp. 167–78.

Bell, C. (1988), 'Credit Markets and Interlinked Transactions', in H. Chenery and T.N. Srinivasan (eds), *Handbook of Development Economics*, North Holland: Amsterdam.

Bell, C. (1990), 'Interactions between Institutional and Informal Credit Agencies in Rural India', *World Bank Economic Review*, Vol. 4, pp. 297–327.

Bencivenga, V.R. and B.D. Smith (1991), 'Financial Intermediation and Endogenous Growth', *Review of Economic Studies*, Vol. 58, pp. 195–209.

Bencivenga, V.R., B.D. Smith and R.M. Starr (1996), 'Equity Markets, Transactions Cost and Capital: An Illustration', *World Bank Economic Review*, Vol. 10, pp. 241–65.

Benston, G.J. and G.G. Kaufman (1997), 'FDICIA after Five Years', *Journal of Economic Perspectives*, Vol. 11, pp. 139–58.

Bernanke, B.S. and M. Gertler (1989), 'Agency Costs, Collateral, and Business Fluctuations', *American Economic Review*, Vol. 79, pp. 14–31.

Besanco, D. and A.V. Thakor (1987), 'Collateral and Rationing: Sorting Equilibria in Monopolistic and Competitive Credit Markets', *International Economic Review*, Vol. 28, pp. 671–89.

Bester, H. (1985), 'Screening vs. Rationing in Credit Markets with Imperfect Information', *American Economic Review*, Vol. 73, pp. 850–55.

Bester, H. (1995), 'A Bargaining Model of Financial Intermediation', *European Economic Review*, Vol. 39, pp. 211–28.

Bhaduri, A. (1973), 'A Study in Agricultural Backwardness under Semi-feudalism', *Economic Journal*, Vol. 83, pp. 120–37.

Bhaduri, A. (1977), 'On the Formation of Usurious Interest Rates in

Backward Agriculture', *Cambridge Journal of Economics*, Vol. 1, pp. 34–52.

Bhaduri, A. (1987), 'Dependent and Self-reliant Growth with Foreign Borrowing', *Cambridge Journal of Economics*, Vol. 11, pp. 269–73.

Bhaduri, A. (1990), *Macro-economics: The Dynamics of Commodity Production*, revised Indian edition: Macmillan, first published in 1986.

Bhagwati, J. (1998a), 'The Capital Myth: The Difference between Trade in Widgets and Dollars', *Foreign Affairs*, Vol. 77, May/June, pp. 7–12.

Bhagwati, J. (1998b), 'The Design of Indian Development', in I.J. Ahluwalia and I.M.D. Little (eds) *India's Economic Reforms and Development Essays for Manmohan Singh*, Delhi: Oxford University Press.

Bhagwati, J.N. and P. Desai (1970), *India, Planning for Industrialisation*, London: Oxford University Press.

Bhatt, V.V. and A.R. Roe (1979), *Capital Market Imperfections and Economic Development*, World Bank Staff Working Papers No. 338, Washington, DC: The World Bank.

Bhattacharya, S. and A.V. Thakor (1993), 'Contemporary Banking Theory', *Journal of Financial Intermediation*, Vol. 13, pp. 2–50.

BIE (1981), *Finance for Small Business Growth and Development*, Bureau of Industry Economics, Canberra: AGPS.

BIE (1985), *Small Business Review*, Bureau of Industry Economics, Canberra: AGPS.

Blinder, A. and J.E. Stiglitz (1983), 'Money Credit Constraint and Economic Activity', *American Economic Review*, Vol. 73, pp. 297–302.

Bloomfield, A.I. (1992), 'On the Centenary of Jacob Viner's Birth: A Retrospective View of the Man and his Work', *Journal of Economic Literature*, Vol. 30, pp. 2052–85.

Bolton, J.E. (1972), *Small Firms: Report of the Committee of Inquiry on Small Firms*, London: HMSO.

Bottomley, A. (1964), 'Monopoly Profit as a Determinant of Interest Rates in Underdeveloped Rural Areas', *Oxford Economic Papers*, Vol. 16, pp. 431–7.

Bottomley, A. (1965), 'Reply', *Quarterly Journal of Economics*, Vol. 79, pp. 325–7.

Bottomley, A. (1975), 'Interest Rates Determination in Underdeveloped Rural Areas', *American Journal of Agricultural Economics*, Vol. 57, pp. 279–91.

Boulding, K.E. (1962), *Conflict and Defence A General Theory*, New York: Harper Torch Books.

Brandenburger, A. and E. Dekel (1990), 'The Role of Common Knowledge Assumptions in Game Theory', in F. Hahn (ed.), *The Economics of Missing Markets, Information and Games*, Oxford: Clarendon Press.

Calomiris, C.W. and R.G. Hubbard (1990), 'Firm Heterogeneity, International Finance, and Credit Rationing', *Economic Journal*, Vol. 100, pp. 90–104.

Calomiris, C.W. and J.R. Mason (1997), 'Contagion and Bank Failures during the Great Depression: The June 1932 Chicago Banking Panic', *American Economic Review*, Vol. 87, pp. 863–83.

Campbell Committee (1981), *Committee of Inquiry into the Australian Financial System,* Canberra: AGPS.

Capiro, G. and P. Honohan (1999), 'Restoring Banking Stability: Beyond Supervised Capital Requirements', *Journal of Economic Perspectives*, Vol. 13, pp. 43–64.

Caves, R. and M. Uekusa (1976), 'Industrial Organisation', in H. Patrick and H. Rosovsky (eds) *Asia's New Giant: How the Japanese Economy Works,* Washington, DC: The Brooking Institution.

Chakravarty, S. (1987a), 'Marxist Economics and Contemporary Developing Economies', *Cambridge Journal of Economics*, Vol. 11, pp. 3–32.

Chakravarty, S. (1987b), *Development Planning: The Indian Experience*, Oxford: Oxford University Press.

Chakravarty, S. (1993a), 'Theory of Development Planning: An Appraisal', in S. Chakravarty, *Selected Economic Writings*, Delhi: Oxford University Press.

Chakravarty, S. (1993b), 'Report of the Committee to Review the Working of the Monetary System – A Re-examination', in S. Chakravarty, *Selected Economic Writings*, Delhi: Oxford University Press.

Chandavarkar, A.G. (1971), *Some Aspects of Interest Rate Policies in Less Developed Economies: The Experience of Selected Asian Economies*, IMF Staff Papers, March, Washington, DC: IMF.

Chandavarkar, A. (1992), 'Of Finance and Development: Neglected and Unsettled Questions', *World Development*, Vol. 20, pp. 133–42.

Chase, S.B. Jr (1960), 'The Lock-in Effect: Bank Reactions to Securities Losses', *Monthly Review*, Federal Reserve Bank of Kansas City, June, pp. 283–9.

Chase, S.B. Jr (1961), 'Credit Risk and Credit Rationing: Comment', *Quarterly Journal of Economics*, Vol. 75, pp. 319–29.

Cho, Y. Je (1988), 'The Effect of Financial Liberalisation on the Efficiency of Credit Allocation: Some Evidence from Korea', *Journal of Development Economics*, Vol. 29, pp. 101–10.

Cho, Y. Je (1989), 'Finance and Development: The Korean Approach', *Oxford Review of Economic Policy*, Vol. 5, pp. 88–102.

Choong-Hwan, R. (1990), 'Korean Corporate Financing', *Monthly Review*, Korean Exchange Bank, April, Vol. 24, pp. 3–13.

Coase, R. (1977), 'The Wealth of Nations', *Economic Inquiry*, Vol. 15, pp. 309–25.

Cole, D. and Y.C. Park (1983), *Financial Development in Korea, 1945–1978*, Cambridge: Harvard University Press.

Corbo, V. and J. De Melo (1985), 'Overview and Summary', *World Development*, Vol. 13, pp. 863–6.

Coveney, P. and R. Highfield (1991), *The Arrow of Time: The Quest to Solve Science's Greatest Mystery*, London: Flamingo.

Dasgupta, A. (1993), *A History of Indian Economic Thought*, London: Routledge.

Dasgupta, S. (1970), *Agriculture: Producer's Rationality and Technical Change*, Delhi: Asia Publishing House.

Datta-Chaudhuri, M. (1990), 'Market Failure and Government Failure', *Journal of Economic Perspectives*, Vol. 4, pp. 25–39.

Davies, P. (1995), *The Cosmic Blueprint: Order and Complexity at the Edge of Chaos*, Harmondsworth: Penguin Books.

De Gregorio, J. and P.E. Guidotti (1995), 'Financial Development and Economic Growth', *World Development*, Vol. 23, pp. 433–48.

Demetriades, P.O. and K.B. Luintel (1996), 'Financial Development, Economic Growth and Banking Sector Controls: Evidence from India', *Economic Journal*, Vol. 106, pp. 359–74.

De Meza, D. and D. Webb (1987), 'Too Much Investment: A Problem of Asymmetric Information', *Quarterly Journal of Economics*, Vol. 102, pp. 281–92.

De Meza, D. and D. Webb (1999), 'Wealth, Enterprise and Credit Policy', *Economic Journal*, Vol. 109, pp. 153–63.

Desai, M. (1998), 'Development Perspectives: Was there an Alternative to Mahalanobis?', in I.J. Ahluwalia and I.M.D. Little (eds) *India's Economic Reforms and Development Essays for Manmohan Singh*, Delhi: Oxford University Press.

Devereux, M.B. and G.W. Smith (1994), 'International Risk Sharing and

Economic Growth', *International Economic Review*, Vol. 35, pp. 535–50.

Diamond, D.W. (1984), 'Financial Intermediation and Delegated Monitoring', *Review of Economic Studies*, Vol. 51, pp. 393–414.

Diaz-Alejandro, C.F. (1985), 'Good-bye Financial Repression, Hello Financial Crash', *Journal of Development Economics*, Vol. 19, pp. 1–24.

Dornbusch, R. and A. Reynoso (1989), 'Financial Factors in Economic Development', *American Economic Review*, Vol. 79, pp. 204–9.

Dougherty, C. (1980), *Interest and Profit*, London: Methuen & Co. Ltd.

Edwards, F.R. (1999), 'Hedge Funds and the Collapse of Long Term Capital Management', *Journal of Economic Perspectives*, Vol. 13, pp. 189–210.

Eshag, Eprime and M.A. Kamal (1967), 'A Note on the Reform of the Rural Credit System in UAR (Egypt)', *Bulletin of the Oxford University of Economics and Statistics*.

Fama, E. (1980), 'Banking in the Theory of Finance', *Journal of Monetary Economics*, Vol. 6, pp. 7–28.

Fei, J.C.H. (1960), 'The Study of the Credit System by the Method of Linear Graph', *Review of Economics and Statistics*, Vol. 42, pp. 417–28.

Fellner, W. (1960), 'Appraisal of Recent Tight-money Policies', *Review of Economics and Statistics*, Vol. 42, pp. 252–5.

Fields, G.S. (1984), 'Employment, Income Distribution and Economic Growth in Seven Small Open Economies', *Economic Journal*, Vol. 94, pp. 74–83.

Fisher, I. (1932), *Booms and Depressions*, New York: Adelphi.

Freimer, M. and M. Gordon (1965), 'Why Bankers Ration Credit', *Quarterly Journal of Economics*, Vol. 79, pp. 397–416.

Friedman, M. (1971), 'The Euro-dollar Market: Some First Principles', *Federal Reserve Bank of St. Louis*, July, pp. 16–24.

Fry, M.J. (1978), 'Money and Capital or Financial Deepening in Economic Development?' *Journal of Money Credit and Banking*, Vol. 10, pp. 464–75.

Fry, M.J. (1980), 'Saving, Investment, Growth and the Cost of Financial Repression', *World Development*, Vol. 8, pp. 317–27.

Fry, M.J. (1995), *Money, Interest and Banking in Economic Development*, 2nd edn, Baltimore: Johns Hopkins University Press.

Fry. M.J. (1997), 'In Favour of Financial Liberalisation', *Economic Journal*, Vol. 107, pp. 754–70.

Galbraith, J.A. (1963), *The Economics of Banking Operations*, Montreal, McGill University Press.

Gale, W.G. (1989), *Collateral Rationing and Government Intervention in Credit Markets*, NBER Working Paper No. 3083, Cambridge, MA: NBER.

Garegnani, P. (1978), 'Notes on Consumption, Investment and Effective Demand: I', *Cambridge Journal of Economics*, Vol. 2, pp. 335–53.

Garegnani, P. (1979), 'Notes on Consumption, Investment and Effective Demand: II', *Cambridge Journal of Economics*, Vol. 3, pp. 63–82.

Georgescu-Roegen, N. (1971), *The Entropy Law and the Economic Process*, Cambridge, MA: Harvard University Press.

Gertler, M. and A. Rose (1994), 'Finance, Public Policy and Growth', in G. Capiro, I. Atiyas and J. Hansen (eds) *Financial Reform: Theory and Experience*, New York: Cambridge University Press.

Gertler, M.L. (1992), 'Financial Capacity and Output Fluctuations in an Economy with Multi-period Financial Relationships', *Review of Economic Studies*, Vol. 59, pp. 455–72.

Gertler, M.L. and S.G. Gilchrist (1994), 'Monetary Policy, Business Cycles, and the Behaviour of Small Manufacturing Firms', *Quarterly Journal of Economics*, Vol. 109, pp. 309–40.

Ghatak, S. (1995), *Monetary Economics in Developing Countries*, 2nd edn, New York: St. Martin's Press.

Giovannini, A. (1983), 'The Interest Elasticity of Savings in Developing Countries: The Existing Evidence', *World Development*, Vol. 11, pp. 601–7.

Giovannini, A. (1985), 'Savings and the Real Interest Rate in LDCs', *Journal of Development Economics*, Vol. 18, pp. 197–217.

Goldsmith, R.W. (1969), *Financial Structure and Development*, New Haven, CT: Yale University Press.

Goodhart, C.A.E. (1995), *The Central Bank and the Financial System*, London: Macmillan.

Greene, J. and D. Villanueva (1991), 'Private Investment in Developing Countries', *IMF Staff Papers*, Vol. 38, pp. 33–58.

Greenwood, J. and B. Jovanovic (1990), 'Financial Development, Growth, and the Distribution of Income', *Journal of Political Economy*, Vol. 98, pp. 1076–1108.

Grey, A.L. Jr and M.D. Brockie (1959), 'The Rate of Interest, Marginal Efficiency of Capital and Investment Programing – A Rejoinder', *Economic Journal*, Vol. 69, pp. 333–43.

Gribbin, J. (1999), *Schrodinger's Kittens and the Search for Reality*, London: Phoenix, first published in 1995.

Griffin, K. (1974), *The Political Economy of Agrarian Change*, London: Macmillan.

Gupta, K.L. (1987), 'Aggregate Savings, Financial Intermediation and Interest Rates', *Review of Economics and Statistics*, Vol. 69, pp. 303–11.

Gupta, S.B. (1988), *Monetary Economics: Institutions, Theory and Policy*, New Delhi: S. Chand and Co.

Gurley, J.G., H.T. Patrick and E.S. Shaw (1965), 'The Financial Structure of Korea', Draft, United States Operations Mission to Korea.

Haavelmo, T. (1954), *A Study in the Theory of Economic Evolution*, Amsterdam: North Holland.

Hahn, F. (1985), *Money, Growth and Stability*, Oxford: Basil Blackwell.

Hahn, F. (1990a), 'Introduction', in F. Hahn (ed.), *The Economics of Missing Markets, Information and Games*, Oxford: Clarendon Press.

Hahn, F. (1990b), 'Information Dynamics and Equilibrium', in F. Hahn (ed.) *The Economics of Missing Markets, Information and Games*, Oxford: Clarendon Press.

Hall, M.J.B. (1992), 'Implementation of the BIS "Rules" on Capital Adequacy Assessment', *Banca Nationale Del Lavoro Quarterly Review*, March, pp. 35–45.

Hansen, A.H. (1960), 'Appropriate Monetary Policy, 1957–60', *Review of Economics and Statistics*, Vol. 42, pp. 255–61.

Harris, S.E. (1960), 'Controversial Issues in Recent Monetary Policy: A Symposium', *Review of Economics and Statistics*, Vol. 42, pp. 245–7.

Harshanyi, J.C. (1967–68), 'Games with Incomplete Information Played by Bayesian Players', *Management Science*, Vol. 14, pp. 159–82, 320–34 and 486–502.

Hart, A.G. (1949), 'Keynes' Analysis of Expectations and Uncertainty', in S.E. Harris (ed.) *The New Economics: Keynes' Influence on Theory and Public Policy*, 2nd impression, London: Dennis Dobson Ltd.

Hawtrey, R.G. (1944), *Economic Destiny: The End and the Means of Welfare or Power Work or Chaos*, London: Longmans, Green and Co.

Hawtrey, R.G. (1962), *The Art of Central Banking*, Frank Cass and Co. Ltd, first published in 1932.

Hayek, F.A. (1939), 'Price Expectations, Monetary Disturbances and

Malinvestment', in *Profits, Interest and Investment*, London: Routledge and Sons.

Heal, G. (1977), 'Guarantees and Risk Sharing', *Review of Economic Studies*, Vol. 44, pp. 549–60.

Heisenberg, W. (1930), *The Physical Principles of the Quantum Theory*, translated by C. Eckart and F.C. Hoyt, Chicago: Chicago University Press.

Heisenberg, W. (1958), *Physics and Philosophy: The Revolution in Modern Science*, New York: Harper.

Hellmann, T.F., K.C. Murdock and J.E. Stiglitz (2000), 'Liberalization, Moral Hazard in Banking, and Prudential Regulation: Are Capital Requirements Enough?' *American Economic Review*, Vol. 90, pp. 147–65.

Hicks, J.R. (1979), *Critical Essays in Monetary Theory*, Oxford: Clarendon Press.

Hodgman, D.R. (1959), 'In Defence of the Availability Doctrine: A Comment', *Review of Economics and Statistics*, Vol. 41, pp. 70–73.

Hodgman, D.R. (1960), 'Credit Risk and Credit Rationing', *Quarterly Journal of Economics*, Vol. 74, pp. 258–78.

Hodgman, D.R. (1961), 'The Deposit Relationship and Commercial Bank Investment Behaviour', *Review of Economics and Statistics*, Vol. 43, pp. 257–68.

Hodgman, D.R. (1962), 'Reply', *Quarterly Journal of Economics*, Vol. 76, pp. 488–9.

Jaffee, D.M. (1971), *Credit Rationing and the Commercial Loan Market*, New York: John Wiley.

Jaffee, D.M. and F. Modigliani (1969), 'A Theory and Test of Credit Rationing', *American Economic Review*, Vol. 59, pp. 850–72.

Jaffee, D.M. and T. Russell (1976), 'Imperfect Information, Uncertainty and Credit Rationing', *Quarterly Journal of Economics*, Vol. 90, pp. 651–66.

Jaffee, D.M. and J.E. Stiglitz (1990), 'Credit Rationing', in B.M. Friedman and F.H. Hahn (eds) *Handbook of Monetary Economics*, Vol. 1, Amsterdam: Elsevier, pp. 837–88.

Jappelli, T. (1990), 'Who is Credit Constrained in the US Economy?', *Quarterly Journal of Economics*, Vol. 105, pp. 219–34.

Jaramillo, F., F. Schiantarelli and A. Weiss (1996), 'Capital Market Imperfection Before and After Financial Liberalization: An Eular Equation Approach to Panel Data for Ecuadorian Firms', *Journal of Development Economics*, Vol. 51, pp. 367–86.

Jensen, M. and W. Meckling (1976), 'Theory of the Firm: Managerial Behaviour, Agency Costs, and Ownership Structure', *Journal of Financial Economics*, Oct, pp. 305–60.

Johns, B.L., W.C. Dunlop and W.J. Sheehan (1983), *Small Business in Australia: Problems and Prospects*, Sydney: George Allen and Unwin.

Jones, L.P. and I.I. Sakong (1980), *Government Business and Entrepreneurship in Economic Development: The Korean Case*, Cambridge, MA: Harvard University Press.

Juttner, D.J and R.G. Bird (1976), 'Financial Problems of Small Firms in the Manufacturing Sector: The Australian Case', *Kredit Und Capital*, Heft-3, pp. 384–415.

Kaldor, N. (1961), 'Capital Accumulation and Economic Growth', in F.A. Lutz and D.C. Hague (eds) *The Theory of Capital*, London: Macmillan, pp. 177–222.

Kalecki, M. (1971), *Selected Essays on the Dynamics of the Capitalist Economy*, Cambridge: Cambridge University Press.

Kaminsky, G.L. and C.M. Reinhart (1999), 'The Twin Crises: The Causes of Banking and Balance of Payments Problems', *American Economic Review*, Vol. 89, pp. 473–500.

Kane, E.J. and B.G. Malkeil (1965), 'Bank Portfolio Allocation, Deposit Variability, and the Availability Doctrine', *Quarterly Journal of Economics*, Vol. 79, pp. 113–34.

Kareken, J.H. (1957), 'Lenders' Preferences, Credit Rationing, and the Effectiveness of Monetary Policy', *Review of Economics and Statistics*, Vol. 39, pp. 292–302.

Karkal, G.L. (1967), *Unorganized Money Markets in India*, Bombay: Lalvani Publishing House.

Keeton, W.R. (1979), *Equilibrium Credit Rationing*, New York and London: Garland Publishing.

Keynes, J.M. (1930), *Treatise on Money*, Vol. II, London: Macmillan and Co Ltd, reprinted in 1965.

Keynes, J.M. (1936), *General Theory of Employment Interest and Money*, London: Macmillan/Cambridge University Press, for the Royal Economic Society, reprinted in 1981.

Keynes, J.M. (1973), *The General Theory and After, Part II, Defence and Development, Collected Writings of J.M. Keynes*, Vol. XIV, London: Macmillan Press.

Khandker, S., B. Khalily and Z. Khan (1995), *Grameen Bank: Performance and Sustainability*, World Bank Discussion Paper No. 306, Washington, DC: The World Bank.

Khatkhate, D. (1988), 'Assessing the Impact of Interest Rates in Less Developed Countries', *World Development*, Vol. 16, pp. 513–42.

Kim, J.C. (1985), 'The Markets for "Lemons" Reconsidered: A Model of the Used Car Market with Asymmetric Information', *American Economic Review*, Vol. 75, pp. 836–43.

Kim, K.S. (1991), 'The Interest-rate Reform of 1965 and Domestic Savings', in Lee-Jay Cho and Kim Yoon Hyung (eds) *Economic Development in the Republic of Korea: A Policy Perspective*, An East-West Centre Book, Honolulu, HI: The University of Hawaii Press.

Kindleberger, C. (1989), *Manias, Panics and Crashes*, 2nd edn, London: Macmillan.

King, R.G. and R. Levine (1993a), 'Finance and Growth: Schumpeter Might be Right', *Quarterly Journal of Economics*, Vol. 108, pp. 717–37.

King, R.G. and R. Levine (1993b), 'Finance, Entrepreneurship, and Growth: Theory and Evidence', *Journal of Monetary Economics*, Vol. 32, pp. 513–42.

Knight, F.J. (1921), *Risk, Uncertainty and Profit*, Boston and New York: Houghton Mifflin Company.

Kregel, J.A. (1978), *The Reconstruction of Political Economy: An Introduction to Post-Keynesian Economics*, 2nd edn, London: The Macmillan Press, reprinted 1975.

Krishnaswamy, K.S., K. Krishnamurty and P.D. Sharma (1987), *Improving Domestic Resource Mobilisation through Financial Development: India*, Manila: Asian Development Bank.

Kuznets, S. (1954), *Economic Change; Selected Essays in Business Cycles, National Income, and Economic Growth*, London: William Heinemann Ltd.

Kuznets, S. (1955), 'Towards a Theory of Economic Growth', in R. Levachman (ed.) *National Policy for Economic Welfare at Home and Abroad*, New York: Doubleday and Co, pp. 12–85.

Lall, S. (1994), 'The East Asian Miracle: Does the Bell Toll for Industrial Strategy?', *World Development*, Vol. 22, pp. 645–54.

Lall, S. (1997), 'Paradigms of Development: A Rejoinder', *Oxford Development Studies*, Vol. 25, pp. 245–53.

Lawson, T. (1985), 'Uncertainty and Economic Analysis', *Economic Journal*, Vol. 95, pp. 909–27.

Lee, S.J. (1997), 'Financial Crisis in Korea', mimeograph, Yale University, New Haven, CT.

Levine, R. (1992), *Financial Structure and Economic Development*, Working Paper WPS.849, Washington, DC: World Bank.

Levine, R. and S. Zervos (1996), 'Stock Market Development and Long-run Growth', *World Bank Economic Review*, Vol. 10, pp. 323–39.

Levine, R. and S. Zervos (1998), 'Stock Markets, Banks, and Economic Growth', *American Economic Review*, Vol. 88, pp. 537–58.

Levitsky, J. (1983), 'Assessment of Bank Small Scale Enterprise Lending', World Bank Industry Department, Washington, DC, processed 1983.

Lindbeck, A. (1962), *The 'New' Theory of Credit Control in the United States*, 2nd edn, Stockholm: Stockholm Economic Studies.

Little, I.M.D., D. Mazumdar and J.M. Page, Jr (1987), *Small Manufacturing Enterprises: A Comparative Analysis of India and Other Countries*, A World Bank Research Publication, Oxford: Oxford University Press.

Lucas, R.E. Jr (1988), 'On Mechanics of Economic Development', *Journal of Monetary Economics*, Vol. 22, pp. 3–42.

Lutz, F.A. (1945), 'The Interest Rate and Investment in a Dynamic Economy', *American Economic Review*, Vol. 35, pp. 811–30.

Machina, M.J. (1987), 'Choice Under Uncertainty: Problems Solved and Unsolved', *Journal of Economic Perspectives*, Vol. 1, pp. 121–54.

McKinnon, R.I. (1973), *Money and Capital in Economic Development*, Washington, DC: Brooking Institutions.

McKinnon, R.I. (1991), *The Order of Liberalization Financial Control in the Transition to a Market Economy*, Baltimore: The Johns Hopkins University Press.

Marshall, A. (1920), *Principles of Economics*, 8th edn, London: Macmillan, reprinted in 1982.

Mathieson, D.J. (1980), 'Financial Reform and Stabilization Policy in Developing Economy', *Journal of Development Economics*, Vol. 7, pp. 359–95.

Matthews, R.C.O. (1954), *A Study in Trade Cycle History*, Cambridge: Cambridge University Press.

Mayer, C. (1988), 'New Issues in Corporate Finance', *European Economic Review*, Vol. 32, pp. 1167–1188.

Mellor, L.W. (1968), 'The Evolution of Rural Development Policy', in L.M. Mellor, J. Weaver, U. Lele and M. Simon (eds) *Developing Rural India*, Bombay: Lalvani.

Meltzer, A.H. (1988), *Keynes' Monetary Theory: A Different Interpretation*, Cambridge: Cambridge University Press.

Mikesell, R.F. and J.E. Zinser (1972), 'The Nature of the Savings Function in Developing Countries: A Survey of the Theoretical and Empirical Literature', *Journal of Economic Literature* , Vol. 11, pp. 1–26.

Milgrom, P.R. and J. Roberts (1987), 'Informational Asymmetries, Strategic Behaviour and Industrial Organisations', *American Economic Review*, Vol. 77 (papers and proceedings), pp. 184–93.

Miller, M.H. (1962), 'Further Comment', *Quarterly Journal of Economics*, Vol. 76, pp. 480–88.

Ministry of International Trade and Industry (MITI) (1983), *Outline of Small and Medium-scale Enterprise Policies of the Japanese Government*, Tokyo: Small and Medium Enterprise Agency, MITI, January.

Minsky, H.P. (1957), 'Central Banking and Money Market Changes', *Quarterly Journal of Economics*, Vol. 71, pp. 171–87.

Minsky, H.P. (1977), 'A Theory of Systematic Fragility', in E.I. Altman and A.W. Sametz (eds) *Financial Crisis: Institution and Markets in a Fragile Environment,* New York: Wiley International.

Miskin, F.S. (1999), 'Global Financial Instability: Framework, Events, Issues', *Journal of Economic Perspectives*, Vol. 13, pp. 3–20.

Modigliani, F. (1963), 'The Monetary Mechanism and Its Interaction with Real Phenomena', *Review of Economics and Statistics*, Vol. 45, pp. 79–107.

Modigliani, F. (1986), 'Life Cycle, Individual Thrift, and the Wealth of Nations', *American Economic Review*, Vol. 76, pp. 297–313.

Modigliani, F. and M.H. Miller (1958), 'The Cost of Capital, Corporation Finance and the Theory of Investment', *American Economic Review*, Vol. 48, pp. 261–97.

Morisset, J. (1993), 'Does Financial Liberalization Really Improve Private Investment in Developing Countries?' *Journal of Development Economics*, Vol. 40, pp. 133–40.

Myers, S.C. and N.S. Majluf (1984), 'Corporate Financing and Investment Decisions when Firms Have Information and Investors Do Not Have', *Journal of Financial Economics*, Vol. 13, pp. 187–221.

Myrdal, G. (1968), *Asian Drama: An Inquiry into the Poverty of Nations*, Vol. 2, New York: Pantheon.

Nagaraj, R. (1996), *India's Capital Market Growth: Trends, Explanations and Evidence*, New Delhi: Indira Gandhi Institute of Development Research.

Nisbet, C. (1967), 'Interest Rates and Imperfect Competition in the Informal Credit Market of Rural Chile', *Economic Development and Cultural Change*, Vol. 16, October.

Nurkse, R. (1953), *Problems of Capital Formation in Under-developed Countries*, Oxford: Oxford University Press.

O'Brien, P.F. and F. Browne (1992), *A 'Credit Crunch?' The Recent Slowdown in Bank Lending and Its Implications for Monetary Policy*, Economics and Statistics Department Working Papers No. 107, Paris: OECD.

Obstfeld, M. (1994), 'Risk-taking, Global Diversification and Growth', *American Economic Review*, Vol. 84, pp. 1310–29.

Ojha, P.D. (1982), 'Finance for Small-scale Enterprise in India', *Reserve Bank of India Bulletin*, November.

Osmani, S. (1995), 'The Entitlement Approach to Famine: An Assessment', in K. Basu, P. Pattanaik and K. Suzumura (eds) *Choice, Welfare and Development: A Festschrift in Honour of Amartya K. Sen*, Oxford: Clarendon Press.

Pais, A. (1991), *Neils Bohr's Times, in Physics, Philosophy and Polity*, Oxford: Clarendon Press.

Park, Y.C. (1985), 'Korea's Experience with External Debt Management', in G. Smith and J. Cuddington (eds) *International Debt and the Developing Countries*, Baltimore, MD: Johns Hopkins University Press.

Passinetti, L. (1981), *Structural Change and Economic Growth: A Theoretical Essay on the Dynamics of the Wealth of Nations*, Cambridge: Cambridge University Press.

Passinetti, L. (1993), *Structural Economic Dynamics: A Theory of the Economic Consequences of Human Learning*, Cambridge: Cambridge University Press.

Philips, L. (1988), *The Economics of Imperfect Information*, Cambridge: Cambridge University Press.

Pindyck, R.S. (1991), 'Irreversibility, Uncertainty, and Investment', *Journal of Economic Literature*, Vol. 29, pp. 1110–48.

Prasad, P.H. (1974), 'Limits to Investment Planning', in Ashok Mitra (ed.) *Economic Theory and Planning: Essays in the Honour of A.K. Dasgupta*, Delhi: Oxford University Press.

Radelet, S. and J. Sachs (1998), 'The East Asian Financial Crisis: Diagnosis, Remedies and Propects', *Brookings Papers on Economic Activity*, No. 1, pp. 1–90.

Raj, K.N. (1979), 'Keynesian Economics and Agrarian Economics', in C.H. Hanumantha Rao and P.C. Joshi (eds) *Reflections on Economic Development and Social Change: Essays in Honour of Professor V.K.R.V. Rao*, Bombay: Allied Publishers.

Rajan, R.G. and L. Zingales (1998), 'Financial Dependence and Growth', *American Economic Review*, Vol. 88, pp. 559–86.

Renfrew, K.M., W.J. Sheehan and W.C. Dunlop (1985), *Financing and Growth of Small Business in Australia*, Contributed paper-2, Bureau of Industry Economics (BIE), Canberra: AGPS.

Report of the President (1982), *The State of Small Business: A Report of the President*, Washington, DC: Government Printing, March.

Reserve Bank of India (1969), *Report of the All-India Rural Credit Review Committee*, Bombay: RBA.

Reserve Bank of India (1979), *Report of the Working Group to Review the System of Cash Credit*, Bombay: RBA.

Reserve Bank of India (1987a), *All-India Debt and Investment Survey 1981–82 (Assets and Liabilities of Households as on 30th of June 1981)*, Bombay: RBA.

Reserve Bank of India (1987b), *All-India Debt and Investment Survey 1981–82 (Statistical Tables Relating to Capital Expenditure and Capital Formation of Households during the year ended 30th of June 1982)*, Bombay: RBA.

Riley, J. (1987), 'Credit Rationing: A Further Remark', *American Economic Review*, Vol. 77, pp. 224–31.

Robinson, E.A.G. (1931), *The Structure of Competitive Industry*, Cambridge Economic Handbooks, Cambridge: Cambridge University Press.

Robinson, J. (1979), 'The Generalisation of the General Theory', in *The Generalisation of the General Theory and Other Essays*, 2nd edn, London: Macmillan.

Robinson, J. (1980), *Further Contributions to Modern Economics*, Oxford: Basil Blackwell.

Roe, A.R. (1982), 'High Interest Rates: A New Conventional Wisdom for Development Policy? Some Conclusions from Sri Lankan Experience', *World Development*, Vol. 10, pp. 211–22.

Romer, P. (1986), 'Increasing Returns to Scale and Long-run Growth', *Journal of Political Economy*, Vol. 94, pp. 1002–37.

Romer, P. (1990), 'Endogenous Technical Change', *Journal of Political Economy*, Vol. 98, pp. S71–S102.

Roosa, R.V. (1951), 'Interest Rates and the Control Bank', in *Money Trade and Economic Growth: in Honour of John Henry Williams*, New York: Macmillan Co.

Roosa, R.V. (1960), 'The Changes in Money and Credit, 1957–59', *Review of Economics and Statistics*, Vol. 42, pp. 261–3.

Rosenstein-Rodan, P.N. (1943), 'Problems of Industrialisation in Eastern and South-Eastern Europe', *Economic Journal*, Vol. 53, pp. 202–11.

Roth, H.D. (1979), 'Money Lenders' Management of Loan Agreement: Report on a Case Study in Dhanbad', *Economic and Political Weekly*, 14 July.

Roubini, N. and X. Sala-i-Martin (1992), 'Financial Repression and Economic Growth', *Journal of Development Economics*, Vol. 39, pp. 5–30.

Rudra, A. (1975), *Indian Plan Models*, Delhi: Allied Publishers.

Rudra, A. (1992), *Political Economy of Indian Agriculture*, Calcutta: K.P. Bagchi and Company.

Ryder, J.R. (1962), 'Credit Risk and Credit Rationing: Comment', *Quarterly Journal of Economics*, Vol. 76, pp. 471–9.

Saint-Paul, G. (1992), 'Technological Choice, Financial Markets and Economic Development', *European Economic Review*, Vol. 36, pp. 763–81.

Samuelson, P.A. (1960), 'Reflections on Monetary Policy', *Review of Economics and Statistics*, Vol. 42, pp. 263–9.

Samuelson, P.A. (1966), 'An Appraisal of Mathematics', in J.E. Stiglitz (ed.) *Collected Scientific Papers of Paul A. Samuelson*, Vol. II, Cambridge: MIT Press.

Sayers, R.S. (1949), 'Central Banking in the Light of Recent British and American Experience', *Quarterly Journal of Economics*, Vol. 63, pp. 198–211.

Sayers, R.S. (1960a), *Modern Banking*, 5th edn, Oxford: Clarendon Press.

Sayers, R.S. (1960b), 'Monetary Thought and Monetary Policy in England', *Economic Journal*, Vol. 70, pp. 710–24.

Scherer, F.M. (1980), *Industrial Market Structure and Economic Performance*, 2nd edn, Chicago: Rand McNally College, Publishing Company.

Scitovsky, T. (1940), 'A Study of Interest and Capital', *Economica*, Vol. 7, pp. 304–6.

Scitovsky, T. (1954), 'Two Concepts of External Economies', *Journal of Political Economy*, Vol. 62, pp. 143–51.

Scott, Ira O. Jr (1957a), 'The Availabilty Doctrine: Theoretical Underpinning', *Review of Economic Studies*, Vol. 25, pp. 41–8.

Scott, Ira O. Jr (1957b), 'The Availability Doctrine: Development and Implications', *Canadian Journal of Economics and Political Science*, Vol. 23, pp. 532–9.

Sen, A.K. (1981), *Poverty and Famine: An Essay on Entitlement and Deprivation*, Oxford: Clarendon Press.

Sen, A.K. (1983), 'Development: Which Way Now?' *Economic Journal*, Vol. 93, pp. 745–62

Sen, A.K. (1984a), 'On Optimizing the Rate of Saving', *Economic Journal*, Vol. 71, 1961, reprinted in *Resources, Value and Development*, Oxford: Basil Blackwell.

Sen, A.K. (1984b), 'Approaches to the Choice of Discount Rates for Social Benefit–Cost Analysis', in R. Lind (ed.) *Discounting for Time and Risk in Energy Policy*, 1982, reprinted in A.K. Sen (ed.) *Resources, Values and Development*, Oxford: Basil Blackwell.

Sen, K. and Vaidya, R. (1997), *The Process of Financial Liberalization in India*, Delhi: Oxford University Press.

Shackle, G.L.S. (1946), 'Interest Rates and the Pace of Investment', *Economic Journal*, Vol. 56, pp. 1–17.

Shaw, E. (1973), *Financing Deepening in Economic Development*, New York: Oxford University Press.

Singh, A. (1993), 'The Stock Market and Economic Development: Should Developing Countries Encourage Stock Markets?' *UNCTAD Review*, No. 4, pp. 1–28.

Singh, A. (1994), 'Openness and the Market Friendly Approach to Development: Learning the Right Lessons from Development Experience', *World Development*, Vol. 22, pp. 1811–23.

Singh, A. (1995), *Corporate Financial Patterns in Industrialising Economies: A Comparative International Study*, IFC Technical Paper No. 2, Washington, DC: World Bank.

Singh, A. (1997), 'Financial Liberalisation, Stock Markets and Economic Development', *Economic Journal*, Vol. 107, pp. 771–82.

Singh, A. (1998), 'Liberalization, the Stock Market, and the Market for Corporate Control: A Bridge too Far for the Indian Economy?' in I.J. Ahluwalia and I.M.D. Little (eds) *India's Economic Reforms and Development Essays for Manmohan Singh*, Delhi: Oxford University Press.

Sinkey, J.F. (1989), *Commercial Bank Financial Management in the Financial Services Industry*, 3rd edn, New York: Macmillan.

Smith, A. (1776), *An Inquiry into the Nature and Causes of the Wealth of Nations*, E. Cannan (ed.), New York: The Modern Library, 1937.

Smith, L.E.D., M. Stockbridge and H.R. Lohano (1999), 'Facilitating the Provision of Farm Credit; The Role of Interlocking Transactions between Traders and Zamindars in Crop Market System in Sindh', *World Development*, Vol. 27, pp. 403–18.

Smith, W.L. (1956), 'On the Effectiveness of Monetary Policy', *American Economic Review*, Vol. 46, pp. 566–606.

Smith, W.L. (1960), 'Monetary Policy, 1957–1960: An Appraisal', *Review of Economics and Statistics*, Vol. 42, pp. 269–72.

Solow, R.M. (1957), 'Technical Change and the Aggregate Production Function', *Review of Economics and Statistics*, Vol. 39, pp. 312–20.

Srinivasan, T.N. (1998), 'India's Export Performance: A Comparative Analysis', in I.J. Ahluwalia and I.M.D. Little (eds) *India's Economic Reforms and Development Essays for Manmohan Singh*, Delhi: Oxford University Press.

Srinivasan, T.N. (2000), *Eight Lectures on India's Economic Reforms*, Oxford: Oxford University Press.

Stern, N. (1989), 'The Economics of Development: A Survey', *Economic Journal*, Vol. 99, pp. 597–685.

Stiglitz, J.E. (1985), 'Credit Markets and the Control of Capital', *Journal of Money, Credit and Banking*, Vol. 17, pp. 133–52.

Stiglitz, J.E. (1992), 'Introduction – S&L Bail-out', in J.R. Bath and R.D. Brumbaugh (eds) *The Reform of the Federal Deposit Insurance: Disciplining the Government and Protecting the Taxpayers*, New York: Harper Collins.

Stiglitz, J.E. (1993), 'The Role of the State in Financial Markets', *World Bank Economic Review* (Proceedings of the Annual Conference on Development Economics), pp. 19–52.

Stiglitz, J.E. and A. Weiss (1981), 'Credit Rationing in Markets with Imperfect Information', *American Economic Review*, Vol. 71, pp. 393–410.

Stiglitz, J.E. and A. Weiss (1987), 'Credit Rationing: Reply', *American Economic Review*, Vol. 77, pp. 228–31.

Storey, D.J. (1982), *Entrepreneurship and The New Firm*, London: Croom Helm.

Streeten, P. (1981), *Development Perspective*, London: Macmillan.

Sundarajan, V. and Thakur, S. (1980), 'Public Investment, Crowding Out and Growth: A Dynamic Model Applied to India and Korea', *IMF Staff Papers,* December, Washington, DC: IMF.

Taylor, L. (1983), *Structuralist Macroeconomics*, New York: Basic Books Inc.

Taylor, L. (1997), 'Editorial: The Revival of the Liberal Creed the IMF and the World Bank in a Globalized Economy', *World Development*, Vol. 25, pp. 145–52.

Tendulkar, S.D. (1998), 'Indian Economic Policy Reforms and Poverty: An Assessment', in I.J. Ahluwalia and I.M.D. Little (eds) *India's Economic Reforms and Development Essays for Manmohan Singh*, Delhi: Oxford University Press.

Thomas, W. (1960), 'How Much Can Be Expected of Monetary Policy?' *Review of Economics and Statistics*, Vol. 42, pp. 272–76.

Thomson, J. and D. Leyden (1982), 'The United States of America', in D.J. Storey (ed.) *The Small Firm: An International Survey*, London: Croom Helm.

Tobin, J. (1953), 'Monetary Policy and the Management of the Public Debt: The Patman Inquiry', *Review of Economics and Statistics*, Vol. 35, pp. 118–27.

Tobin, J. (1960), 'Towards Improving the Efficiency of the Monetary Mechanism', *Review of Economics and Statistics*, Vol. 42, pp. 276–9.

Tobin, J. (1984), 'On the Efficiency of the Financial System', *Lloyds Bank Review*, July, pp. 1–15.

U. Tan, Wai. (1957), 'Interest Rates Outside the Organized Money Markets of Under-developed Countries', *International Monetary Fund, Staff Papers*, Vol. 16, November.

van Wijnbergen, S. (1983), 'Credit Policy, Inflation and Growth in a Financially Repressed Economy', *Journal of Development Economics*, Vol. 13, pp. 45–65.

Viner, J. (1937), *Studies in the Theory of International Trade*, New York: Harper & Brothers.

Vittas, D. and Y. Je Cho (1996), 'Credit Policies: Lessons from Japan and Korea', *World Bank Research Observer*, Vol. 11, pp. 277–98.

Wade, R. (1998), 'From "Miracle" to "Cronyism" in the Asian Crisis', *Cambridge Journal of Economics*, Vol. 22, pp. 693–706.

Wallich, H.C. (1953), 'Recent Monetary Policies in the United States', *American Economic Review*, Vol. 43, pp. 27–41.

Weintrub, S. (1960), 'Monetary Policy, 1957–59: Too Tight, Too Open', *Review of Economics and Statistics*, Vol. 42, pp. 279–82.

Westphal, L. (1990), 'Industrial Policy in an Export-propelled Economy: Lessons from South Korea's Experience', *Journal of Economic Perspectives*, Vol. 4, pp. 41–59.

White, W.H. (1956), 'Interest Inelasticity of Investment Demand – The

Case from Business Attitude Surveys Re-examined', *American Economic Review*, Vol. 46, pp. 565–87.

White, W.H. (1958), 'The Rate of Interest, the Marginal Efficiency of Capital and Investment Programming', *Economic Journal*, Vol. 68, pp. 51–9.

Williamson, S.D. (1986), 'Costly Monitoring, Financial Intermediation, and Equilibrium Credit Rationing', *Journal of Monetary Economics*, Vol. 18, pp. 159–79.

Wilson, Sir Harold (1979), *Studies of Small Firms' Financing*, Research Report No. 3, December, London: Committee to Review the Functioning of Financial Institutions.

Wilson, J.S. (1954), 'Credit Rationing and the Relevant Rate of Interest', *Economica*, Vol. 21, pp. 21–31.

Wilson, T. and P.W.S. Andrews (1951), *Oxford Studies in the Price Mechanism*, Oxford: Clarendon Press.

World Bank (1989), *World Development Report 1989*, New York: Oxford University Press.

World Bank (1993), *The East Asian Miracle*, New York: Oxford University Press.

Wydick, B. (1999), 'Can Social Cohesion be Harnessed to Repair Market Failures? Evidence from Group Lending in Guatemala', *Economic Journal*, Vol. 109, pp. 463–75.

Index

NEW DIRECTIONS IN MODERN ECONOMICS

Post-Keynesian Monetary Economics
New Approaches to Financial Modelling
Edited by Philip Arestis

Keynes's Principle of Effective Demand
Edward J. Amadeo

New Directions in Post-Keynesian Economics
Edited by John Pheby

Theory and Policy in Political Economy
Essays in Pricing, Distribution and Growth
Edited by Philip Arestis and Yiannis Kitromilides

Keynes's Third Alternative?
The Neo-Ricardian Keynesians and the Post Keynesians
Amitava Krishna Dutt and Edward J. Amadeo

Wages and Profits in the Capitalist Economy
The Impact of Monopolistic Power on Macroeconomic Performance in
the USA and UK
Andrew Henley

Prices, Profits and Financial Structures
A Post-Keynesian Approach to Competition
Gokhan Capoglu

International Perspectives on Profitability and Accumulation
Edited by Fred Moseley and Edward N. Wolff

Mr Keynes and the Post Keynesians
Principles of Macroeconomics for a Monetary Production Economy
Fernando J. Cardim de Carvalho

The Economic Surplus in Advanced Economies
Edited by John B. Davis

Foundations of Post-Keynesian Economic Analysis
Marc Lavoie

The Post-Keynesian Approach to Economics
An Alternative Analysis of Economic Theory and Policy
Philip Arestis

Income Distribution in a Corporate Economy
Russell Rimmer

The Economics of the Profit Rate
Competition, Crises and Historical Tendencies in Capitalism
Gérard Duménil and Dominique Lévy

Corporatism and Economic Performance
A Comparative Analysis of Market Economies
Andrew Henley and Euclid Tsakalotos

Competition, Technology and Money
Classical and Post-Keynesian Perspectives
Edited by Mark A. Glick

Investment Cycles in Capitalist Economies
A Kaleckian Behavioural Contribution
Jerry Courvisanos

Does Financial Deregulation Work?
A Critique of Free Market Approaches
Bruce Coggins

Pricing Theory in Post Keynesian Economics
A Realist Approach
Paul Downward

The Economics of Intangible Investment
Elizabeth Webster

Globalization and the Erosion of National Financial Systems
Is Declining Autonomy Inevitable?
Marc Schaberg

Explaining Prices in the Global Economy
A Post-Keynesian Model
Henk-Jan Brinkman

Capitalism, Socialism, and Radical Political Economy
Essays in Honor of Howard J. Sherman
Edited by Robert Pollin

Financial Liberalisation and Intervention
A New Analysis of Credit Rationing
Santonu Basu